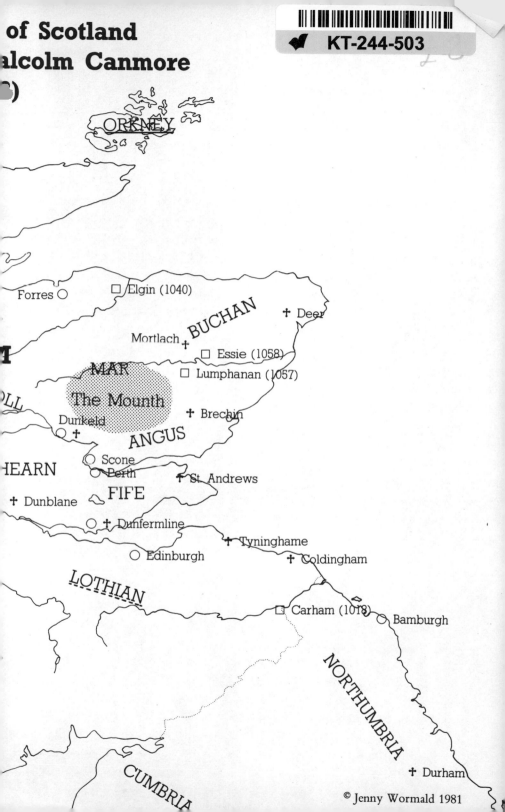

ORKNEY

Forres ○   □ Elgin (1040)

BUCHAN   † Deer

Mortlach †   □ Essie (1058)

□ Lumphanan (1057)

MAR

The Mounth

Dunkeld ○ †   † Brechin

ANGUS

HEARN   ○ Scone

○ Perth   † St Andrews

† Dunblane   ⌒ FIFE

○ † Dunfermline

○ Edinburgh   † Tyninghame

† Coldingham

LOTHIAN

□ Carham (1018) ○ Bamburgh

NORTHUMBRIA

CUMBRIA   † Durham

© Jenny Wormald 1981

THE FLOWER OF SCOTLAND

A History of Scottish Monarchy
Professor James J. Sharp

with an introduction by
Professor Gordon Donaldson

THE FLOWER OF SCOTLAND

A History of Scottish Monarchy
Professor James J. Sharp

with an introduction by
Professor Gordon Donaldson

MELVEN PRESS

Perth, 1981

ISBN 0 906664 10 1

Published by the Melven Press,
176, High Street, Perth, Scotland

The publisher would like to acknowledge the considerable assistance given by Norman Reid in his painstaking selection of suitable photographs; Professor Gordon Donaldson for his advice; John Bartholomew and Sons Ltd., Edinburgh for their help in selecting an endpaper map; Dr Jenny Wormald of Glasgow University for preparing a map especially for this publication; the National Library of Scotland, the Scottish Development department, the National Museum of Antiquities of Scotland, Durham Dean and Chapter Library, the Scottish Record Office, the National Gallery of Scotland, Archives Nationales, Paris, the Royal Commission on the Ancient Monuments, of Scotland, and to the Duke of Buccleuch and Queensbury, K.T., for their respective permission to reproduce the photographs which appear in this book.

Printed in Scotland by Bookmag,
Henderson Road, Inverness.

To
Dorothy, Helen and Eddie

CONTENTS

GENEALOGIES

List of Black and White Illustrations

FOREWORD

The last twenty or thirty years have been a period of unprecedented output of writings on Scottish history, many of them the authoritative results of exact and thorough research. Yet it is notorious that it takes a long time for the findings of scholars to filter through to the popular mind, and indeed I have often remarked that a good error never seems to die. It is certainly noticeable that almost every time a newspaper ventures into history it makes a howler. There is therefore always room for the single-volume comprehensive survey which makes the truth available to all.

Professor Sharp has produced a singularly useful book. He has read the scholarly works and presents their substance in simple and clear language, in a volume which is well-proportioned and is at once readable and a book of easy reference. The fact that he is not himself a professional historian but works in fields which habituate him to high standards of precision is much in his favour. He can appreciate what the non-historian looks for. Besides, both his own professional experience and his residence on the other side of the Atlantic have the advantage of giving him the all-important quality of detachment.

Gordon Donaldson, 1980

THE BIRTH OF THE NATION

When the Roman Legions finally retreated from North Britain, they left behind a land which had never been quite subdued despite a number of deep and testing invasions. Within 130 years of Julius Caesar's first steps on the South coast, the armies of Julius Agricola were pushing northwards and, by AD 80, Roman influence extended as far as the Forth estuary. Forts were established between the rivers Forth and Clyde (possibly under the later Antonine Wall) and a forward, expansionist policy was in being. With the intention of subduing the Caledonians in the North, and so consolidating and securing those gains already made in the South, Agricola set out to expand his system of forts and extend the rudimentary road network. In AD 82 he marched into Ayrshire and Galloway. In the following year he advanced up the East coast to Stonehaven and, by AD 84, his armies had reached the Moray Firth. There, for the first time, the Caledonians abandoned their guerilla tactics and faced up to the legions in a large set piece battle. The site of the conflict, Mons Graupius, is still obscure but the event was perhaps remembered when the Grampian Mountains received their name. After a resounding victory the Roman legions withdrew slowly but the fleet sailed on to subdue the Orkneys and to demonstrate that Britain was an island.

The Roman fort was no mean affair. Inchtuthil in Perthshire, for example, was more like a fortified city than a simple military outpost. Surrounded by a stone wall over 2000 yards long, it was designed to contain, "sixty-four large barracks, four tribune's houses, six granaries, a hospital,

3

workshop and drill hall". In total, Agricola was responsible for at least twenty forts in Scotland south of the Forth and nine or ten north of the Forth. Inchtuthil, one of the last to be built, was never completed because, when Agricola was recalled in AD 84, the empire changed to a more defensive policy. Forts in forward regions were abandoned and, within 40 years, the legions were entrenched behind the large stone wall constructed on the orders of the emperor Hadrian. This, however, seems to have been too far south to suit military needs, because, soon after Antonius Pius arrived in the province, it was decided that a new defensive line must again be established between the Forth and Clyde estuaries.

Antonine's wall (122-128) was 37 miles long and somewhat similar to Hadrian's but was built of turf rather than stone. On the north side the wall was protected by a large ditch, forty feet wide and twelve feet deep. A stone base provided suitable foundations on which the turf rose to a height of about nine feet, being surmounted by a walkway and wooden palisades. Eighteen forts, at intervals of about two miles, were constructed along its length.

Turbulent years followed. Risings behind Hadrian's wall necessitated the recall of troops to the south and, with insufficient strength to man the forward frontier, Antonine's wall was abandoned. It was reoccupied again when the rebellion was quelled but only for a short time before a final retirement in 163. Towards the end of the century renewed attacks on Hadrian's wall prompted further Roman incursions into the north and the emperor Severus mounted a campaign, between 208 and 209, in which the legions marched into Angus. This was relatively successful and the third century remained fairly peaceful. Roman strength was maintained at Hadrian's Wall and a careful watch was kept on the Caledonians by scouting parties established in a few forward positions. Another campaign, this time into Perthshire, was organised when trouble broke out again in the early fourth century. But by this time the Roman hold was weakening. In 367 Picts and Scots poured over Hadrian's wall to plunder the rich land to the south. By 400 the wall was abandoned and, within ten years, the province of Britain had been left to look after its own defence as best it could.

There was no single year in which the legions formally departed. Over a long period, men were recalled for other duties and, as the army became weaker, local tribes were incorporated into the system as auxiliaries or 'foederati'. These took on greater and greater responsibility for defending the frontiers so that there was a gradual transition from Roman to local defence.

Throughout the next few hundred years the Island Province descended into what has become known as the Dark Ages. In the South, Romanised Britons, under legendary chiefs like Arthur (c 500), struggled unsuccessfully to repel the Germanic invaders. In the North the four peoples who remained when the Romans departed gradually coalesced to become the Scottish Nation.

Records for the 6th and 7th century show that a warrior society existed among the Picts, Scots, Britons and Angles. Wealth was counted in cattle and other moveable goods and there was constant feuding, more in pursuit of treasure than for the purpose of acquiring territory. The boundaries of the kingdoms varied but, in general, the Picts inhabited the North and East, and presumably the North West. Britons, who had become somewhat more civilised, lived in the South but were pushed out of the South East by Angle invasions from Northumbria. Thereafter, they were largely confined to the kingdom of Strathclyde in the South West. The Scots, from whom the nation was to take its name, settled along the west coast in Kintyre and Argyll but did not penetrate north of Skye which seems to have remained in Pictish hands.

Tall and red haired, the Picts are first mentioned in Roman sources of 297. The origin of their name is not fully understood and it may simply come from the latin 'picti' meaning painted people. They are thought to be the original inhabitants of the land and there is no doubt that they formed the strong core around which the Scottish monarchy grew and prospered. Legend traces their origin back to the land of

Scythia from which they journeyed to the North of Scotland. Being without women on their travels they were provided with wives by the Scots in Ireland on condition that the line of descent would pass down through the female rather than the male side of the family. In fact, irrespective of its origin, the Picts, alone among the people of North Europe, did practise matrilinear descent in which the right to be king descended through the female line.

It seems probable that they were divided into two groups; the Southern Picts and the Northern Picts. In 565 the Pictish king, Brudei, resided at a hill fort on the River Ness but in later years the Picts' strength was concentrated more in the Southern part of the kingdom and the capital was eventually situated at Scone. The prefix 'pit', in towns such as Pitlochry, has Pictish origins and their name itself survives in the Pentland (Pictland) hills and the Pentland firth.

The Scots formed part of the barbarian onslaught which weakened the Roman empire and led to its eventual demise. From their kingdom in Antrim on the northern coast of Ireland, they sailed to Britain in skin and wooden boats via the Southern Hebrides and, around 500, established three settlements; in Kintyre, around Oban, and in Isla and Jura. The people called themselves the Dal Riata and this name was soon transferred to their Scottish kingdom, Dalriada. Irish myths suggest that they were descended from Gaythelos, (hence Gael) a prince of Greece, and that they had arrived in Ireland via Egypt and Spain. Throughout these journeys the Scots carried with them a sacred stone believed to be Jacob's pillow and ultimately to become known as the Stone of Scone. It is said to have been held at Iona and at forts on Loch Etive before being taken to Scone.

The most famous Scot was no doubt Columba, a princely churchman, who was exiled from Ireland in 563. Arriving in Iona he set up a small Christian community, reinforced the faith already present among the Scots and sent out missions to the Northern Picts. His influence and prestige rallied the Scots, who at that time were disunited, but after his death the power and strength of Dalriada fell into decay. Nevertheless it was a Scottish king, Kenneth MacAlpin, who united these two people in 843, after which the land was called Alba.

Britons, in the South had been more strongly influenced by the Roman presence than any of the peoples to the North. They had a loose aristocratic society, lived in towns and villages and farmed the fertile low lying land. The Votadini, in the East, were first to experience the attacks which were to reduce the British kingdom to impotence. Pirate ships invaded from the North Sea but much more serious was the pressure exerted by the Angles, Germanic invaders who had become established in Northumbria. Moving up the East coast of Scotland, the Angles conquered the country around Edinburgh, which is thought to have taken its name from Edwin, a king of the Angles who lived in the early fifth century. British influence on the East coast waned and was later confined to the kingdom of Strathclyde, or Cumbria, i.e. South West Scotland and Cumberland.

In times of peace the border between Briton and Angle may have been quite clearly defined and remains of rudimentary earthworks have been discovered in Southern Scotland and in the North of England. Although too small for defensive purposes, the earth walls which ran between the various rivers would have been quite adequate to prevent cattle crossing and were probably useful in preventing unauthorised border raiding.

Peace was fragile, however, and the Britons were constantly subjected, not only to pressure from the Angles in the South, but also to raids from the Scots and to attacks by the Vikings. In 870, the capital of Strathclyde, Dumbarton, was sacked by Irish Danes and the kingdom was then gradually assimilated into Alba. From the early tenth century Strathclyde was a client state of the king of Scots and was finally incorporated into the youthful nation in 1034 when Duncan I, already ruler in Strathclyde, succeeded to the Scottish throne.

Around the same time, the power of the English in the South East also waned. Invasions from Scandinavia cut off the northern Angles from their relations in the South and internal dissentions were rife. Edinburgh was ceded to the Scots at the end of the eighth century when the Norse kingdom of York was finally brought under the control of an English king. In 1018 Malcolm II was victorious over Earl Uhtred of Bamburgh at the battle of Carham after which the English under Cnut (Canute) ceded the land North of the Tweed in return for a secure peace.

What caused the people of Scotland to unite? Certainly much was achieved by force of arms but the four peoples, originally so distinct, grew to have much in common. The Roman legacy to Scotland had indicated the strength of a united front compared to that of minor kingdoms which had been unable to overcome internal feuds. Attacks by Vikings and the power struggle in England made alliances necessary for survival, but perhaps the strongest bond was that of Christianity. Parts of Northern Britain were nominally Christian before the Romans left but the conversion of Scotland was achieved largely as a result of the work of Ninian and Columba. Ninian, a Briton, established his see at Whithorn around 400 and led missions to the Southern Picts. Columba, arriving from Christian Ireland 150 years later, settled in Iona and converted the Northern Picts. From these two centres missionaries travelled throughout the country and, by the middle of the eighth century, most of Scotland was Christian.

From 843, when Kenneth MacAlpin united the Scots and the Picts, until 1034, when Duncan ruled over a United Scotland, sources describe a sorry tale of continual internal feuding and almost constant Viking attacks. Throughout this period and, in line with the practice in Ireland, the king was chosen from a 'Royal' kinship group any of whom could claim to be the most suitable ruler. For almost two hundred years the choice bounced back and forwards among three, and then two, families. The reversal of this practice, when Duncan I succeeded his grandfather, Malcolm II, may have been largely instrumental in causing the rebellion by Macbeth who had a claim to the throne through his wife and also, perhaps, in his own right.

Little is known of kings of Alba, their appearance or character, until Macbeth was killed and succeeded by Malcolm III (Canmore). None of them had a good biographer (Macbeth was treated most unfairly by Shakespeare) and the few details which are available must be gleaned from old Irish annals or from ancient historians such as Bede and Adamnan. Nevertheless, the pattern of development is fairly clear. Kenneth MacAlpin never ruled south of the Pentland Hills. His son, Constantine, lost the North and West to the Vikings and, for a long time, Alba extended only over Eastern Scotland from the Moray Firth to the River Forth. Over the years Strathclyde was assimilated and Lothian was added, largely through the inability of the Anglo Saxon kings to exercise effective control over this, their most northerly province. Then in 1018, Malcolm II's victory at Carham pushed the border south to the Solway and the Tweed. Thus, by the time of Macbeth, the last of these shadowy rulers, Alba's southern boundary was set in roughly the same position as that of modern Scotland. The Western Isles and the North would not be recovered until the eleventh century when the House of Canmore was nearing its eclipse.

THE EARLY KINGS

Kenneth MacAlpin — Kenneth III (843-1005)

Relatively little information is available for this period and sources are often confused and contradictory. However, some details are available.

Kenneth, son of Alpin, was king of Scots Dalriada for two years before he united the Picts and Scots in the land called Alba. The throne of Dalriada came to him in 841 when his father was killed in a raid on Galloway. Two years later the king of the Picts died and Kenneth, whose grandmother had been a Pictish princess, claimed the throne of Pictavia. He had to fight to make good his claim but was successful, apparently by attacking the Picts when they were under pressure from Vikings while he was being reinforced from Ireland.

The new country was strengthened by alliances forged through the marriage of Kenneth's daughters to the Kings of Ireland and of Strathclyde. However, it is doubtful if such alliances were of much value. Alba suffered from severe raids, not only by Vikings, but also by Britons who burned Dunblane. Kenneth, who never ruled south of the Pentland hills, raided Northumbria in his search for booty on at least six occasions and is known to have devastated and burned the town of Dunbar. His capital was situated at Dunkeld where he built a church to house the sacred relics of Columba brought over from Iona where he, himself, was buried.

Kenneth was succeeded by his brother Donald I and then

13

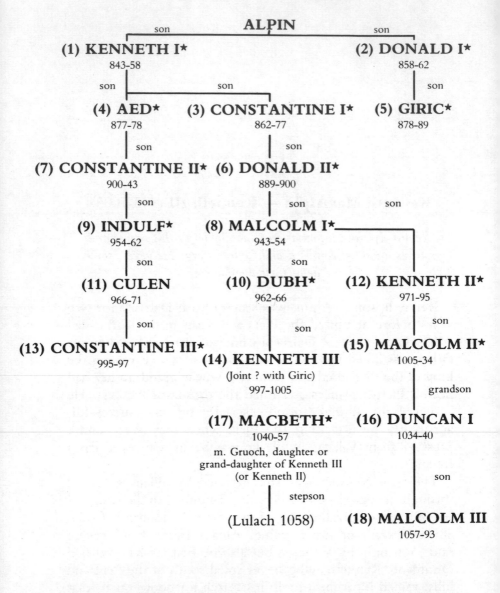

ALPIN

son   son

(1) KENNETH I★
843–58

(2) DONALD I★
858–62

son   son   son

(4) AED★
877–78

(3) CONSTANTINE I★
862–77

(5) GIRIC★
878–89

son   son

(7) CONSTANTINE II★
900–43

(6) DONALD II★
889–900

son   son   son

(9) INDULF★
954–62

(8) MALCOLM I★
943–54

son   son

(11) CULEN
966–71

(10) DUBH★
962–66

(12) KENNETH II★
971–95

son   son   son

(13) CONSTANTINE III★
995–97

(14) KENNETH III
(Joint ? with Giric)
997–1005

(15) MALCOLM II★
1005–34

grandson

(17) MACBETH★
1040–57
m. Gruoch, daughter or
grand-daughter of Kenneth III
(or Kenneth II)

(16) DUNCAN I
1034–40

son

stepson

(Lulach 1058)

(18) MALCOLM III
1057–93

★*Buried at Iona*

LINES OF SUCCESSION OF THE EARLY KINGS

by his son Constantine I, a contemporary of Alfred the Great. Viking attacks, which appear to have been absent during Donald's short four years in power, were renewed during this period and, for the first time, the invaders took hostages and exacted tribute. Dumbarton, then capital of Strathclyde, was sacked in 870 and was controlled by the Vikings for several years thereafter. Constantine appears to have been instrumental in the assassination of the puppet king in Strathclyde around 872.

Three years later the Vikings from Orkney invaded Alba to consolidate their hold in the north. Constantine was defeated at Dollar and Caithness and Sutherland were lost to the Scots crown for most of the next three centuries. Norse pressure became somewhat relieved by this agreement but again, in 877, the Vikings descended on Fife, where Constantine was killed when he attempted to repulse them.

Relatively little is known of the twenty-three years following the death of Constantine I. There is evidence of some Viking raids but possibly of most interest is the moving of the capital from Dunkeld to Scone where Scots kings were then crowned for many centuries. This occurred during the reign of Giric, son of Donald I, and may have been due to his desire for a safer capital, farther removed from the raids of the Norse.

Constantine II, grandson of Kenneth MacAlpin, was the first King of Scots to obtain any significant authority south of the river Forth. He ruled for over forty years and appears to have brought Strathclyde more strongly under Scots control by arranging the election of a kinsman to the throne when the King of Strathclyde died in 908. Then, in 920, he further extended his influence after acknowledging the Anglo-Saxon king, Edward, as "father and lord", the first occasion on which kings of Alba placed themselves in a somewhat inferior position relative to the rulers in England. Four years later the treaty was renewed with Edward's successor, Athelstan.

Alba was invaded by Vikings in the early part of Constantine's reign and later (934) by the Anglo-Saxons under Athelstan. As pressures on England grew her enemies joined forces and, in 937, Constantine launched a large scale invasion in conjunction with Owen, King of Strathclyde, and the Irish Norse from Dublin. The result was a catastrophic defeat for the invaders. Constantine lost his son in the battle and fled north with the remnants of his army. Six years later he relinquished the throne (voluntarily?) to become a monk at St Andrews. There he lived for another nine years, reappearing briefly after retirement in 950 to lead the Scots troops after urging his successor, Malcolm I, to once again invade England.

In 939, Viking pressures on England led to the fall of York which was then formally ceded to the Danes. However, with some respite from constant attack, the Anglo-Saxons were able to build up their strength and, in 944, one year after Constantine died, York was recovered by King Edmund. In an effort to secure his Northern border Edmund proceeded to devastate Cumbria (Strathclyde) and then 'let' it to Constantine's successor, Malcolm I, on condition that the Scots king would be "his (Edmund's) helper by land and sea". The bond was later renewed with Edmund's successor but, when York again fell to the Danes in 950, Malcolm took advantage of the confusion by mounting an invasion which ravaged south to the River Tees.

The constant friction between Danes and Anglo-Saxons in the north of England continued to affect the fortunes of Alba and it soon became clear that the early Angles had penetrated too far into Britain for effective control to be exercised from Wessex. Probably as a result, when York was again wrested from the Danes in 954, Edinburgh, lying much further north, was abandoned to the Scots.

The Scottish hold on Lothian was secured some years later during the reign of Kenneth II. Two years after he became King, Kenneth was summoned to attend Edgar, King of the Anglo Saxons, at Chester in order to celebrate the long delayed Saxon coronation. During a lavish water pageant Edgar organized a spectacle in which he took the helm of a boat rowed by Kenneth and seven other Danish, Welsh and

Cumbrian Kings The significance of the act could not have been overlooked by the Scots. Edgar, the great grandson of Alfred the Great, had succeeded in overcoming the problems which had beset England in previous reigns and was bent on preserving the stability which he had worked so hard to achieve. Every king present entered into some sort of treaty with the newly crowned King of England. Kenneth acknowledged him as "lord" and made the now familiar promise to be his "helper by land and sea". In return he was given Lothian provided he agreed to keep the peace.

It appears that Kenneth lived up to his promise, at least until near the end of his reign when there is a possibility that he invaded the north of England. The evidence is not clear. He died in a feud at Fettercairn in 995 caused, perhaps, by his attempts, against all tradition, to secure the succession for his son.

Sources are confused for the years following Kenneth's death but become clearer after Malcolm II killed his predecessor in Monzievaird and seized the throne in 1005.

Malcolm II
Reigned: 1005-1034
Son of Kenneth II
Contemporary of Ethelred, 978-1016
Cnut (Canute), 1016-1035
Buried in Iona

Taking advantage of the renewed Viking problems in England, Malcolm invaded the rich lands of Northumbria in 1006 and may possibly have laid seige to Durham in an attempt to carry off the treasures of St. Cuthbert. However his forces were attacked and defeated by the Earl of Bamburgh. Malcolm was forced to withdraw and gained little for his efforts. Lothian, which was acquired during the reign of Kenneth II, appears to have passed out of Scots control in the latter years of the tenth century or the early years of the eleventh, but was recovered in 1018 when

Malcolm's forces were victorious at the battle of Carham on the river Tweed. No doubt Malcolm took advantage of the confusion in England caused by the triumph of the Danes over the Anglo-Saxons when King Cnut succeeded Ethelred. Although Cnut rose to be one of the most powerful rulers in Europe his position was then insufficiently strong for him to be able to regain control of Lothian.

Malcolm was supported at Carham by Owen the bald, King of Strathclyde, and it seems probable that, from the early tenth century, Strathclyde was effectively a client state of Alba. Certainly, at some time during Malcolm's reign his grandson and successor, Duncan, became King of Strathclyde.

In 1031, when Cnut was at the height of his powers, an invasion of Scotland took place in which the English appear to have reached the Tay. It is possible that the move was undertaken in retaliation for some unwise alliances made by Malcolm, but little is known of the circumstances. The two kings managed to reach an agreement however and peace was maintained.

By the time he died (by assassination or ambush) in 1034 Malcolm had greatly enlarged Alba's sphere of influence. Within thirty years the border had been pushed from the river Forth and the Pentland Hills south to the Solway and the Tweed. Lothian had been brought under Scots control and Strathclyde was only nominally, if at all, independent. Most of the North and West however (Caithness, Sutherland, the Isles, and much of Argyll) remained under the power of the Norse crown and would continue to do so for more than two centuries.

Duncan I
Reigned: 1034-1040
Grandson of Malcolm II through daughter Bethoc married to
Crinan, abbot of Dunkeld
Contemporary of Cnut (1016-1035) and his sons
Married to a cousin of Siward, Earl of Northumbria

Duncan's accession to the throne of Alba was the first instance since the mid ninth century in which the kingship remained in the same family and did not pass to an alternative line. Malcolm II arranged that his grandson, Duncan, would succeed him by ensuring that there were no other significant claimants. By tradition the throne might well have gone to a son of Kenneth III but, during the last years of his reign, Malcolm arranged to have the only surviving son murdered. However, Macbeth, the mormaer (chief steward) of Moray, was married to a woman descended from Kenneth II or Kenneth III. This gave Macbeth a claim to power and the departure from custom occasioned by Duncan's succession may have been the cause of the rebellion which Macbeth led from the semi-autonomous province of Moray. When Duncan marched north to put down the revolt, his position may have been weakened by the heavy losses he had sustained in the preceding year (1039) while attacking Durham. In any event, he was defeated and killed in a battle at Cawdor in 1040. On his death his two sons fled, the elder to his uncle in Northumbria and the younger to the Western Isles.

Macbeth
Reigned: 1040-1057
Son of Findlaech, mormaer of Moray
Contemporary of Edward (the Confessor) 1042-1066
Married to Gruoch, granddaughter of Kenneth III
(or Kenneth II)
Buried in Iona

Macbeth's claim to the throne was based partly on his marriage to Gruoch, the granddaughter of Kenneth III (or possibly Kenneth II) and partly on his own possible descent from a Royal line. Malcolm had arranged the murder of Gruoch's brother to ensure that Duncan (Malcolm's grandson) would succeed him as King and this provided Macbeth with two good reasons for rebellion. By tradition, the throne should have passed into the family of Kenneth III but Gruoch's son by a previous marriage, Lulach the simple, was too young to press his claim. Accordingly when Macbeth married Gruoch, he could press the family claim and at the same time avenge the murder of his wife's brother. As mormaer of Moray he was in a very strong position. From 1020 to 1130 the Irish Annals refer to the rulers of Moray as Kings and it is possible that the province had become almost independent and was, at that time, only nominally under the rule of the Scots Kings.

To quell the revolt which arose in 1040 Duncan marched into Moray but was defeated and killed near Elgin. Macbeth became King in his place and seems to have ruled effectively and well. His reign of seventeen years is much longer than that of most of his predecessors and his seat on the throne was sufficiently secure for him to be able to leave Alba on a visit to Rome in 1050 where he was said to have been very generous to the poor, 'scattering money like seed'. He and Gruoch gave generously to the church and he seems to have been on good relations with Edward the Confessor and the Normans. When Edward was forced to expel his Norman advisors in 1052, two of them fled north and were given sanctuary by Macbeth.

In 1045-46 Macbeth was challenged by Crinan, Abbot of Dunkeld, Duncan's father, and by Earl Siward of Northumbria, a kinsman of Duncan's wife. The challenge was defeated but was renewed eight years later. In July 1054 an invading army marched north from Northumbria. This time it was led by Duncan's son Malcolm who had taken refuge with Siward when his father died at Cawdor. Now a young man, about 23 years old, Malcolm defeated Macbeth and took control over part of the country, probably in the south. However it took another three years to bring Macbeth to a conclusive battle which was fought at Lumphanan in Aberdeenshire. There he was finally defeated and killed. His family's claims to the throne persisted with his stepson Lulach who, in some parts of Alba, was then recognized as King until he, in turn, was killed at Strathbogie in 1058.

With the death of Macbeth the ancient practice of sharing the throne among a number of kinship groups disappeared completely. His successor, Malcolm III, obtained the kingdom only with the aid of foreign (Northumbrian) intervention and established the house of Canmore, alternatively known as the House of Dunkeld since it originated with Crinan, Abbot of Dunkeld. This dynasty was to survive until the end of the thirteenth century and perished when Alexander's horse slipped at Kinghorn.

THE HOUSE OF CANMORE

If the two hundred and fifty years prior to the accession of Malcolm III were dominated by the struggles which formed the infant nation of Scotland, the next quarter century was surely most affected by the ever strengthening ties with England. Malcolm Canmore's second wife was Anglo Saxon and, although little English influence was evident, other than at court, during her lifetime, their sons forged ever closer links with the descendants of William the Conqueror. Of the ten kings who ruled between 1057 and 1286, six married high born English ladies, two were unmarried and one of the remaining two took a wife chosen for him by the King of England. Most owned extensive lands in England, brought to the Royal Family when David I married a great English heiress, and most did homage to an English King for these lands.

The relationship between the two countries was always close but by no means always cordial. On the English side efforts were made to transfer the homage paid by the King of Scots for his English lands into homage for Scotland itself, while the Scots constantly interfered in English civil disturbances and attempted to obtain, by fair means or foul, the rich and tempting provinces in the North of England. However at many times the two kings and their countries were on the most friendly terms and indeed, when the house of Dunkeld reached its eclipse with the death of Alexander III, it may have seemed quite natural to turn to Scotland's good friend, Edward I, for assistance in resolving the disputed succession. Only later would he attempt to

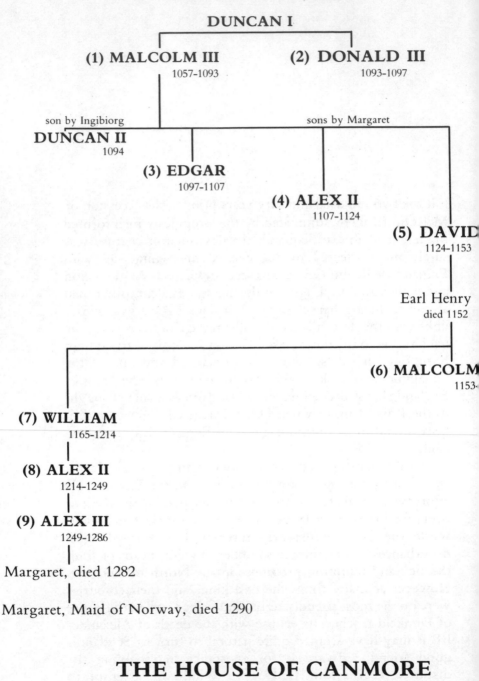

DUNCAN I

(1) MALCOLM III
1057–1093

(2) DONALD III
1093–1097

son by Ingibiorg
DUNCAN II
1094

sons by Margaret

(3) EDGAR
1097–1107

(4) ALEX II
1107–1124

(5) DAVID
1124–1153

Earl Henry
died 1152

(6) MALCOLM
1153–

(7) WILLIAM
1165–1214

(8) ALEX II
1214–1249

(9) ALEX III
1249–1286

Margaret, died 1282

Margaret, Maid of Norway, died 1290

THE HOUSE OF CANMORE

subjugate Scotland to the English crown setting in motion the events which led to the war of independence and which gave him his epitaph, "Hammer of the Scots".

Throughout this period Scotland was gradually consolidated into the geographical boundaries of the present day. The southern frontier was fixed, and the northern mainland, held by the Norse for many years, was regained. In the West, the Isles were brought under the rule of the Scots king and only Shetland and Orkney remained outside Scotland's jurisdiction. The name of the country also changed. When Macbeth died his kingdom was still known as Alba, and Ireland, the native home of the Scots, was called Scotia. This situation continued until about the end of the tenth century when the country of the Scots became known as Scotia and then ultimately as Scotland. The transition was slow and, even as late as the twelfth century, the Bishop of Caithness was observed to complain that, "Alba is now corruptly called Scotland".

Malcolm III (Malcolm Ceann-Mor)
Born c 1031
Reigned 1057-1093
Son of Duncan I
Married —
(1) Ingibiorg, daughter of Thorfinn, Earl of Orkney
(2) Margaret, sister of Edgar the Atheling and granddaughter of Edward the Confessor
Three sons of Ingibiorg; Six sons and two daughters by Margaret
Contemporary of:

Edward (the Confessor)	*1042-1066*
William I (the Conqueror)	*1066-1087*
William II (Rufus)	*1087-1100*

Died at Alnwick
Buried at Dunfermline

Malcolm III (Canmore) whose name means great head or chief, won the throne in 1057, three years after he invaded Scotland with a Northumbrian army. He had fled to his

English uncle when Macbeth defeated his father Duncan, and remained in Northumbria throughout his formative years. When he returned to Scotland in 1054 he quickly won control over part of the kingdom but took three years to bring Macbeth to a conclusive and final battle. Within twelve months of obtaining the throne Malcolm was back in England at the court of the Confessor, possibly to renew the bond of assistance made in earlier times but more probably to argue for the return of English estates previously set aside for the use of the Scots kings.

For over thirty years Malcolm attempted to expand Scots territory by invading the north of England. His first expedition took place in 1061 but appears to have been relatively fruitless. Five years later, following the conquest of England by the Normans, Edgar Atheling, his mother and two sisters fled to Scotland and, in 1070, Malcolm again invaded, taking advantage of the confusion caused by an unsuccessful Saxon revolt. He married Edgar's sister Margaret around 1071 and this, together with the invasion of the previous year, caused William to retaliate. The Conqueror came north with naval support and, at Abernethy, Malcolm made peace "and gave hostages and was his man". It is probable that the King's eldest son Duncan (by Ingibiorg) was among the hostages but Malcolm was not to be deterred for long. The next raid on Northumberland occurred in 1079 and once again resulted in a counter invasion, this time led by Duke Robert, the eldest son of the Conqueror. Robert marched to Falkirk where Malcolm again submitted and renewed the oath. On his return to England Robert decided to strengthen the northern defenses and erected a 'new castle' on the River Tyne. Twelve years later in 1091, after the Conqueror had died and when his successor William Rufus was overseas in Normandy, Malcolm again ravaged the North but had to retreat in haste before an advancing English army led by William and Robert. Although their navy was shipwrecked the Normans penetrated deep into Scotland. Robert mediated between the two kings and Malcolm submitted for the third time. In return for oaths of homage and fealty William promised to return twelve estates in England and make Malcolm an annual payment of 12 merks. Carlisle castle was built in the following year and peasants were settled in the surrounding area. As this seemed to nullify certain aspects of their agreement, Malcolm, with a guarantee of safe conduct, journeyed to visit the English king at Gloucester. No discussions took place, however, because William refused to see him. In anger the Scots king returned home to raise an army for yet another invasion. It would be his fifth and last expedition. Trapped by the Earl of Northumbria at the River Aln, the Scots were defeated on 13 November 1093. Malcolm was killed in the battle and his eldest son by Margaret sustained a mortal wound.

Malcolm's invasions, and the Norman counter invasions, undoubtedly strained the resources of the kingdom but had few lasting effects. Of much more significance was his marriage to Margaret, the granddaughter of Edward the Confessor. Four of her six sons were given names from the Royal house of Wessex (Edward, Edgar, Edmund and Ethelred) and, during her lifetime, Margaret began to introduce English ways to the Scots court. These English and Norman fashions were to become much stronger as her sons inherited the kingdom and the strengthening ties, through marriages and oaths of fealty, were to bind the two crowns closely together, eventually giving English kings the conviction that Scotland was, or should be, a vassal state of her more powerful neighbour.

Malcolm and Margaret were the first Royal couple to live in the castle at Edinburgh. In the eleventh century the stronghold would be little more than a group of small buildings surrounded by a wooden palisade on the highest part of the rock. However, Margaret's chapel, built in stone by one of her sons, still exists and can be visited within the confines of the modern structure. She was renowned for her piety and, being devoted to the shrine of St. Andrew, provided the 'Queen's ferry', where the Forth Bridges now stand, to carry the faithful across the River Forth.

The Queen was ill when Malcolm left Scotland on his last fatal venture and died within a few days of receiving word of her husband's death. When the news broke, the late King's brother Donald, seized the throne and surrounded the castle, but Margaret's body was carried out under cover of mist and taken to the Abbey of Dunfermline where she was buried alongside her husband.

Donald III (Donald Ban — the fair)

Born c 1033
Reigned 1093-1097
Son of Duncan I, brother of Malcolm III
One daughter
Contemporary of William II (Rufus) 1087-1100
Died in Angus
Buried at Iona

Unlike his brother Malcolm, Donald fled to the Isles when their father was defeated and killed by Macbeth. He has been described as "an incorrigible old Celt" and in November of 1093, when Malcolm III was killed in battle at Alnwick, Donald seized the throne in a popular reaction against the English influence which had crept in since his brother married Margaret. The English, including presumably Malcolm's sons, were driven out but, despite the popularity of this move, Donald's throne was very insecure. In England Malcolm's eldest son, Duncan, received an English and French army in return for swearing oaths of fealty and allegiance. He marched into Scotland and conquered his uncle in May of the following year (1094). However immediately after his success he was beaten in a spontaneous Scots rising against the foreigners he had brought to Scotland. Duncan was permitted to keep the throne and the title of King but only if the English and French were expelled. No sooner had this taken place than Donald, in alliance with his nephew Edmund, instigated another revolt in which Duncan was killed. Donald reassumed the throne, probably in conjunction with Edmund, and reawakened the hostility of William II by entering into a treaty of friendship with the rebel earl of Northumberland. William now assigned the Kingdom of Scotland to Edgar (Margaret's second son) as his vassal. With assistance from his protector, Edgar invaded Scotland and defeated Donald in a pitched battle. Edmund resigned any claims to the throne and became a monk at Montague in the South of England. Donald suffered a much harder fate, being blinded and imprisoned at Rescobie in Angus where he later died. He was buried in Iona.

Duncan II
Born c 1060
Reigned May — November 1094
Son of Malcolm III by his first wife Ingibiorg
Contemporary of William II (Rufus) 1087-1100
Married Octreda, daughter of Earl of Northumbria
One son
Died in the Mearns

Given as hostage to William I in 1072, Duncan was released and knighted when William Rufus became King of England in 1087. In return for offering homage and swearing allegiance to William he was provided with an English and French army which enabled him to defeat his uncle, Donald III, and to obtain the throne in May of 1094. A popular rising forced him to expel his foreign helpers and he was subsequently defeated in a revolt organised by Donald III and his (Duncan's) stepbrother Edmund. He was killed by the Mormaer of the Mearns and died in that area. Scotland's earliest surviving charter dates from his short reign and deals with land grants to the monks of Durham.

Edgar

Born c 1074
Reigned 1097-1107
Fourth son of Malcolm III by Margaret
Unmarried
Contemporary of:
William II (Rufus)   1087-1100
Henry I   1101-1135
Died at Edinburgh
Buried at Dunfermline

In similar fashion to his stepbrother Duncan, Edgar fled to England when his uncle, Donald III, seized the throne after Malcolm III was killed in battle. Following Donald's defeat of Duncan II and his reassumption of the throne in 1094, Edgar was acknowledged by William Rufus as the rightful, but vassal, King of Scots. He is known to have styled himself King as early as April 1095, when he made extensive land grants in Berwickshire to St. Cuthbert's church.

With material assistance from Rufus, Edgar invaded Scotland in 1097, defeated Donald, and took the throne. He remained a loyal vassal of Rufus and carried his sword at the crown wearing ceremony of 1099. The links with the English court were strengthened when Henry I married Edgar's sister, Matilda, in 1100. Two years later Henry arranged the marriage of his other sister, Mary, to the Count of Boulogne. The daughter of this union eventually married King Stephen.

Appearing to care little for his native land Edgar ceded all of the Western Isles, including Iona, the most sacred spot in Alba, to Magnus King of Norway, by the treaty of 1098. Legend states that Magnus also obtained Kintyre by dragging boats overland between two sea lochs but this is unlikely. Edgar died, still unmarried, in Edinburgh castle in 1107. Naming his heirs from his deathbed he divided Scotland between his brothers Alexander and David. Alexander was to rule in the north, in Alba proper, whereas David was given control over the area to the south of the Forth.

Alexander I
Born c 1077
Reigned 1107-1124
Fifth son of Malcolm III and Margaret
Contemporary of Henry I 1100-1135
Married Sybilla, bastard daughter of Henry I
One illegitimate son
Died at Stirling
Buried at Dunfermline

Described as a "lettered and godly man" Alexander was the only layman present when the tomb of St. Cuthbert was opened at Durham in 1104. A good friend of the English King, he was given Henry's illegitimate daughter, described as, "lacking in both modesty and beauty", in marriage and led a contingent of Henry's army in a campaign on Wales. He made serious efforts to bring order to the Scots church and, on his enthronement, filled the bishopric of St. Andrews which had been vacant since 1093.

When he assumed the throne in 1107 it was his wish that his brother David, who had been bequeathed southern Scotland by Edgar, should remain in England as 'brother to the queen'. However, by 1113, reluctantly and under pressure, he gave David Teviotdale, Strathclyde and Lothian to rule as Earl David.

He died peacefully at Stirling in 1124 and was buried at Dunfermline in the Abbey founded by his mother.

David I
Born c 1084
Reigned 1124-1153
Youngest son of Malcolm III and Margaret
Contemporary of:
Henry I   1100-1135
Stephen   1135-1154
Married to Maud, daughter and heiress of Earl of Huntingdon
Three (or four) children, but only one son who did not die in
early youth
Died at Carlisle, 24 May 1153
Buried at Dunfermline

When King Edgar died in 1107 he bequeathed part of Scotland — the south — to David who ruled as Earl David under Alexander I until he, in turn, died in 1124. Like his brothers, David spent his youth in England, and on assuming the throne of Scotland, he set in motion the major influx of Normans and English which would continue throughout the next century and turn Scotland into a feudal state.

His ties with England were strengthened by the close relationship with Henry I (he was his brother-in-law) and by his marriage to the heiress, Maud, which made him one of the greatest barons in England.

A, "sair sanct for the croun", David spent considerable resources on the church, founding many Abbeys, mainly Augustinian and Cistercian. Although he resisted southern pressure to make the Scots church subservient to that of the English, his outlook was largely tempered by the time he had spent at the English court. Normans, English and Flemings were invited to join him in Scotland or moved north in search of the opportunities available to them. The feudalisation of Scotland began with these moves; sheriffdom was created, castles were erected and the justiciary was developed.

Of those to whom David granted lands in Scotland, two were of prime significance by virtue of the importance of their descendants. Robert de Brus, a Norman and grandson of the de Brus who accompanied William I in his conquest of England, became known to David during their joint sojourn at the English court, and, soon after David's inauguration, Robert was awarded extensive lands in Annandale. He became one of the king's most favoured barons. In due course the family changed their name to Bruce, married into the royal line and obtained the crown in the war of independence. Walter Fitzallan, the younger son of a Shropshire lord also came north to join David's service and was granted large estates around the River Clyde. With these he was given the honorific title of Royal Steward which was confirmed and made hereditary in the following reign. As a result, the family name of Fitzallan was discarded in favour of Stewart. His descendants became eligible for the crown when the Sixth High Steward, also Walter, married Marjorie Bruce, daughter of Robert I.

The introduction of 'foreigners' to Scotland did not occur without some Celtic resentment. There were, after all, less than thirty years between David's accession and the popular rising against the English introduced by Duncan II. As in the past, the trouble centered around Moray where Angus, a descendant of Macbeth's stepson Lulach, led a rising which ended in failure in 1130. Four years later David subdued and imprisoned another rebel, Malcolm Macheth, thought to have been the illegitimate son of Alexander I and an ally of the late Angus. In 1142 there was yet a further rebellion, this time led by Wimond, Bishop of the Isles, who claimed to be a son of the Earl of Moray. He also met with failure, but strife in the North did not die out and David's successor would later be troubled by a rising led by the sons of Macheth.

Throughout the early years of his reign King David remained on friendly terms with his neighbours in the South. He himself was a great English lord. He was brother of their Queen and his brother, Alexander I, had been married to Henry's illegitimate daughter. However, on Henry's death in 1135, a dispute arose concerning the English succession.

King Stephen was generally accepted as the rightful heir but, prior to his death, Henry had nominated his daughter, Matilda, the mother of Henry Plantagenet. King David, her uncle, lent support to her claims but his actions may have been influenced more by desire for the rich territory in the North of England, than by a wish to provide aid to his niece. He speedily occupied Cumberland and Northumberland and tricked Carlisle and Newcastle into submitting to him. Negotiations led to peace and a truce but these broke down and, in 1138, David's army was decisively beaten at the Battle of the Standard in the North Riding of Yorkshire. Still he did not desist from his efforts and, when Stephen was captured in 1141, David joined Matilda in London. Both had to flee when Stephen's Queen attacked them at Winchester and David retired in haste to Durham. Thereafter he remained a nominal supporter of Matilda but provided no further material assistance, remaining in the occupied lands of northern England which from then on were relatively quiet. On 24 May 1153 he died peacefully at Carlisle, his favourite residence.

Malcolm IV (the Maiden)
Born 1141
Reigned 1153-1165
Grandson of David I
Contemporary of Henry II 1154-1189 (Thomas à Becket)
Unmarried
Died at Jedburgh
Buried at Dunfermline

Malcolm was only twelve years old when he succeeded to the throne. His father, Earl Henry, had been King David's only son to survive beyond early youth but he died in 1152, one year before the King. Malcolm was then chosen as heir apparent and was conducted round the kingdom by the Earl of Fife to demonstrate his new position as King David's successor. As had become customary, he was inaugurated on the Stone of Destiny, the first occasion on which contemporary evidence is given for the event.

The accession of a minor provided an excellent opportunity for rebellion, and the Celtic unrest which had troubled his grandfather, immediately resurfaced. This time the revolt originated with Somerled, Earl of Argyll and Kintyre. Joining forces with two sons of Malcolm Macheth, he kept the country in a state of near civil war for almost three years until one of Macheth's sons was captured and imprisoned with his father. Somerled then turned his attention to the kingdom of the Isles which at that time was ruled by the King of Man under the protection of the Norwegian crown. After two defeats in two years the Manse King fled and a large part of the Isles passed to Somerled's control. He finally made peace with the Scots King in 1160, three years after Malcolm had released the elder Macheth and created him Earl of Ross.

King Malcolm's formal relations with England began in 1157 when he was summoned South and invested with the honour of Huntingdon. For this earldom he paid homage to Henry but, "saving all his dignity", did not compromise the position of Scotland as some of his ancestors had done. The honour was awarded when he agreed to sign a treaty renouncing his rights to the northern territories of Cumberland and Northumberland. These had been occupied by the Scots in 1135 and had later been assigned to them by Henry in return for David's gift of Knighthood, bestowed on him prior to his acceptance as the first Plantagenet King of England. When Henry demanded their return, Malcolm was a youth of only sixteen years and he 'voluntarily' surrendered them, prudently judging that, "in this matter the King of England had the better of the case, because of the strength of his resources". The following year he again went south to receive his own knighthood at Henry's hands but, owing to some difference between the two kings, he was not knighted until 1159 when he accompanied Henry to the siege of Toulouse. This rapidly developing relationship may have proved too much for Scots dignitaries. Reports of spreading dissatisfaction reached Malcolm at Toulouse and necessitated a speedy return to his kingdom. On his arrival at Perth he was besieged by six of the seven Scots Earls who, for some unknown reason, failed to take him prisoner and were brought to terms with the king by the intervention of the leading clergy. As a result of the insurrection Malcolm was forced to subdue Galloway and led three expeditions into that area before completely eliminating the resistance to his rule.

Between 1160 and 1162 Malcolm entered into various arrangements which gave Scotland close ties with the continent. One sister was married to Conan, Duke of Brittany and another to the Count of Holland. Malcolm, himself, was apparently ready to marry Conan's sister but nothing came of the match. As King Henry laid claim to the duchy of Breton he may well have been concerned at these signs of Malcolm's independence and this probably explains why, in 1163, the Scots king was summoned to Woodstock where he paid homage to Henry's son and gave hostages, including his brother David, to the English monarch.

Malcolm had to sustain yet another invasion of his dominions before the end of his short reign. It originated once again with Somerled who organised a fleet of 160 ships with which he sailed up the River Clyde. However, when he landed with the intention of marching on Glasgow, the local population rose against him and he was beaten and killed in 1164 at Renfrew.

The feudalisation of Scotland, begun in the reign of David I, was continued throughout that of Malcolm and, indeed, cannot be considered complete until about 1220. His grandfather had been particularly generous to the church and Malcolm continued this patronage. The Cistercian Abbey of Coupar Angus was founded in 1162 and David's rejection of an English dominated clergy was reinforced by a request, albeit unsuccessful, for metropolitan status for St. Andrews.

Following a protracted illness, he died at Jedburgh on December 9, 1165 and was taken to Dunfermline for burial. By then the country was at peace and, despite his troubles with Somerled, he seems to have won over the Celtic part of his kingdom, being described in the Ulster Annals as, "the best Christian that was to the Gael on the east side of the sea for almsgiving and fasting and devotion".

William (the Lion)
Born 1143
Reigned 1165-1214
Brother of Malcolm IV and grandson of David I
Contemporary of:

Henry II	*1154-1189*
Richard I (the Lion Heart)	*1189-1199*
John	*1199-1216*

Married to Ermengarde de Beaumont
One son, three daughters and six illegitimate children
Died at Stirling
Buried at Arbroath

With the introduction of Anglo–Norman ways by David I and the consolidation of these ideas by Malcolm IV, William can justifiably be considered as the ruler of what was now a basically feudal state. Red haired, and powerfully built, he had far more in common with the French and English than with his native Celtic lords. During his reign the complaint was voiced that, "the more recent kings of Scots profess themselves to be Frenchmen in their race and manners, language and culture, and, after reducing the Scots to utter servitude, admit only Frenchmen to their friendship and service".

Throughout his long reign his actions were dominated by a desire to recover Northumberland which had been bequeathed to him by David I but subsequently resigned to the English crown by his brother Malcolm. Early in 1166 he visited Henry II to discuss peace and his claim in the North. Together they journeyed to the continent but William returned without having secured any agreement. He may have paid homage for the other lands he held of the English king but Henry refused his demands for Northumberland. During the visit he must have incurred the King's extreme displeasure because it is reported in a private letter that the mere mention of William's name caused Henry to fly into a violent rage, tearing at his clothes, ripping the covers on his couch and even gnawing at handfuls of straw snatched up from the floor.

Four years later William and his brother were both present when Henry II attempted to secure the succession of his son by having the boy crowned as the 'young king'. Both paid homage to the youth and the Scots King again asked for Northumberland but was again refused. In 1173 William joined the rebellion of Henry's sons after demanding Northumberland as the price of his assistance. In alliance with France — the beginning of the Auld Alliance — a Scots army moved into England. William marched through the North but had little effect because, although he started several sieges, he seemed to lack the strength of purpose to carry them through. When news of approaching enemy forces reached him he vacillated and was surprised and captured by Henry's troops at Alnwick on 13 July 1174. Less than two weeks later he was brought before Henry in chains and imprisoned on the Continent. In September the rebel sons made their peace and, in return for his freedom, William signed the Treaty of Falaise, doing homage "for Scotland and for all his other lands" and promising that his barons and his, and their, heirs would do likewise in perpetuity. The price of his release was a total sell out of the kingdom. For the first time in its history Scotland became subject to a feudal superior. Scots towns and castles were given over to Henry and it was intended that the Scottish church should be totally subservient to the English, but the Scots Bishops successfully resisted this. In the event only three castles and towns were occupied by the English who took control of Edinburgh, Berwick and Roxburgh. Edinburgh was returned twelve years later in 1186 when William married Ermengarde, the wife chosen for him by his feudal superior, Henry. In 1188 the Scots offered to pay 4000 merks for the release of the other two towns but their offer was refused.

Henry died, an old and broken man, on 6 July 1189 and was succeeded by his son Richard I (the lion heart). Desperate for money to fund his crusade, Richard agreed to cancel the treaty of Falaise in return for payment of 10,000 merks. All the conditions of the treaty were annulled. The Scots regained their independence, and in addition, William recovered his claim on Northumberland. However, Richard had taken steps to ensure that he could not press the claim because, only a few days before William arrived at the English court, the earldom had been sold to the Bishop of Durham.

During Richard's absence in the Holy Land, England was ruled by John his brother who, when news of Richard's capture arrived, attempted to secure the throne for himself. His attempts to obtain William's support in this venture were spurned and William contributed 2000 merks towards Richard's ransom. By March of 1194 Richard was back in England. William attended his second coronation and again pressed his claim to Northumberland. He was at first refused but, when the Bishop of Durham returned the earldom to the English crown, William immediately lodged an offer of 15,000 merks for it, one and a half times as much as he had paid for Scotland. Richard was agreeable provided he retained control of the castles but, as this would give William the revenue from the lands without political or military control, the offer was withdrawn.

When Richard died in April 1199 and John attempted to secure the throne by taking oaths of allegiance from possible enemies, Willaim again renewed his request. John made no promises but replied that the King of Scots would be satisfied if he kept the peace and did not interfere in English affairs. This William did but, after John had been crowned, he refused to give way to William's demands. Relations between the two kings deteriorated and, in 1209, a crisis was reached when the Scots interfered with the construction of an English castle which was thought to threaten Berwick. Following negotiations it was agreed that the castle would not be completed but, as the price of peace, William had to pay 15,000 merks, "for having the goodwill of King John". He also gave hostages, allowed John to arrange marriages for his daughters and, at long last, relinquished any claim to the northern counties after being promised that these would, in future, be the prerogative of the heir to the Scots throne.

Although Northumberland was continually on his mind and although vast resources were spent and offered in his efforts to acquire it, William was not free of trouble in his native land. Indeed some of his problems resulted directly from these efforts. When he was captured in 1174 the two lords of Galloway returned home from the fighting and drove out or killed the English and French who had settled in their lands. They offered allegiance to Henry who refused to accept it and, William, on his release, quickly descended on them with his army. They were only partly subdued and for the next twelve years Galloway bordered on civil war. In 1179 there was trouble in Ross and William marched North to build two castles in an attempt to put down the insurgents. Two years later he was again in action against Donald MacWilliam, a pretender to the throne who claimed descent from King Duncan II. Donald, encouraged by Harald Maddadson, Earl of Caithness and Moray, raised the North and invaded at the head of a large army. For six years Ross was virtually lost to Scotland until Donald was defeated and killed near Inverness in 1187. Harald Maddadson submitted after a Royal army devastated Thurso in 1197 but still there was trouble and the north was not totally subject to the Scots King until the accession of William's son and heir, Alexander II.

The King's last encounter with the Celtic part of his kingdom occurred in 1211 when he had to again contend with rebellion in Ross. His army was successful in capturing the principal protagonist who was speedily executed. William had no further contact with his native Celts and died on the 4th December, only three years later, at Stirling.

Alexander II
Born 1198
Reigned 1214-1249
Son of William (the lion)
Contemporary of:
King John 1199-1216
Henry III 1216-1272
Married:
(1) Joan, daughter of King John (died 1238)
(2) Marie, daughter of Enguerand, Baron de Couchy in Picardy
One son by Marie, one illegitimate daughter
Died near Oban
Buried at Melrose

Alexander's most significant achievement was the consolidation of mainland Scotland. During his reign the southern border was fixed essentially as it is today and, for the first time in many years, a Scots king exercised effective control in the north. Within weeks of his accession, at the age of sixteen years and three months, fighting broke out in what was to be the last great northern uprising. The MacWilliams, who claimed the throne, and the MacHeths, who claimed Moray, invaded Ross but were speedily defeated by a native Celtic magnate who remained loyal to the king. Thereafter there were minor outbreaks of unrest but never again would there be a determined effort to separate the North from Scots jurisdiction.

The rising was quelled on June 15th 1215, the day on which King John signed the Magna Carta. In addition to the general freedoms specified in the Charter, Alexander was named personally and it was stipulated that, as an English baron himself, he would be treated in the same way as the other Barons and would be awarded whatever rights were due to him. It also promised the release of the Scottish hostages given to John by William I and, although these were indeed given their freedom, little else happened as England drifted into civil war. Alexander took advantage of the unrest to lay claim to "his rights" in Northumberland and, in

October, he laid siege to the castle of Norham where the rebellious baron of Northumbria paid homage to him. It is probable that the twenty-five English barons who were to oversee the execution of the Charter had already judged that he was entitled to the three northern counties but, in November, Alexander broke off the siege and only Carlisle was left in Scottish hands. John moved North to retaliate and the barons of Yorkshire, in fear of their king, allied themselves to Alexander and paid homage to him. However King John continued his march. Entering Scotland in mid January, he burned the towns of Berwick, Haddington, Dunbar and Roxburgh. This success forced Alexander to temporarily abandon his gains in the northern counties and, with an army raised at Edinburgh, he marched on a counter offensive into Cumberland. His efforts met with little success and, within the next few months, many barons submitted to John. Others persuaded Prince Louis of France to join the venture and to come to England to press his claim to the throne. When he arrived in May much of John's authority in the North vanished. Alexander retook Carlisle in August of 1216 and then joined Louis at Dover where he did homage for the northern counties. However John offset their success with a raid on the Midlands and Alexander, concerned at the possible implications for Scotland, returned home about the time John died in October. Henry III, John's son, was crowned soon after and received assistance from the Pope. Louis' supporters, including Alexander, were excommunicated and their lands, including Scotland, were placed under interdict. The following of the French Prince rapidly evaporated and, to forestall a possible English invasion, Alexander led another army into Cumberland. It seems, once again, to have had little effect and was the last hostile army to cross the border for eighty years. In December of 1217, Alexander ordered his men to give up Carlisle and, in return, his excommunication was lifted. Three weeks later he did homage to Henry for the earldom of Huntingdon and for the other lands he held in England.

The next three years were spent in attempts to obtain a

political settlement of the differences between the two kings and this was partially achieved in 1220. As a result Alexander married Henry's sister (John's daughter) Joan on 19 June 1221. A final settlement of the border problem would, however, be delayed until 1237 when Alexander surrendered his claim to the three northern counties by the Treaty of York. In return he obtained the honour of Tynedale and the manor of Penrith.

Alexander's wedding, although it brought peace with England, did nothing to subdue the native problems in Scotland. Immediately after the marriage he was in action to put down trouble in Argyll. Two years later an expedition was led north to Caithness where the Bishop and his assistant were killed in a minor rising instigated by overtaxed peasant farmers. The Bishop had been burned alive by the mob and, in retribution, Alexander is said to have cut off the hands and feet of eighty rioters. For this work the Pope wrote expressing his pleasure and referring enthusiastically to his action as that of the 'champion of God' in Caithness. In 1228 there was yet more trouble in which the lord of Abertarff was killed and part of Inverness was set on fire. Alexander gave an army to the Earl of Buchan who brought order back to Moray and, when the King spent Christmas at Elgin in 1230, the pacification of the North was at last complete. Five years later he was again in action in Galloway in order to put a stop to Gallwegian raids on neighbouring counties. It seems to have taken only a few days to bring peace to the area and the loose independence which this large Celtic province had previously enjoyed was then gradually brought to an end.

In spite of his achievements on the Scottish mainland Alexander must have realised that his possessions in the North and West could not be secured until he had control of the Islands off the west coast. However, it took seven years after his success in Caithness and Inverness to settle the border issue, and additional troubles with the English King occupied him until 1244 when a final settlement was reached. Immediately thereafter he took steps to stabilise the western seaboard and made his first offer to buy the Isles from Haakon, King of Norway, "for refined silver". Haakon refused this offer and continued to repulse the additional offers made to him over the next five years. Then, in 1249, the King of Man drowned and Haakon hastily commissioned Ewan, Lord of Argyll, to rule the isles in his place. Ewan, however, although sympathetic to Norway, was a subject of the Scots King. Angered by his attempt to serve two masters, Alexander marched against him and Ewan, refusing to fight or surrender, fled to Lewis. No further action could be taken because the King fell sick with a fever while his fleet was anchored in Oban Bay. He was carried to the Isle of Kerrera where he died on 8 July 1249. The expedition was then disbanded and the King's body was brought back to the mainland for burial in Melrose Abbey.

Alexander III
Born 1241
Reigned 1249-1286
Son of Alexander II
Contemporary of:
Henry III 1216-1272
Edward I (Hammer of the Scots) 1272-1307
Married:
(1) Margaret, daughter of Henry III and sister of Edward I (died 1275)
(2) Yolande, daughter of Robert, Compte de Dreux
One son, two daughters
Died at Kinghorn
Buried at Dunfermline

Alexander was inaugurated in the summer of 1249, only five days after his father's death. The new king was just eight years old and, although some arguments occurred concerning the enthroning ceremony, no attempt was made to disrupt an orderly transition. The young boy was invested with the royal sword by the Bishop of St. Andrews who gave him the oath. He was then led to a cross in the graveyard of Scone Abbey and was placed on the ancient stone, suitably ornamented with gold and silk cloth for the occasion. The King's robe was placed around his shoulders and, on being consecrated by the Bishop of St. Andrews and the Abbot of Scone, he received the homage of the Scots Lords. In order to strengthen, and confirm, his acceptance by his northern subjects, a Celtic bard then knelt before him and recited the young king's pedigree, tracing it back to Alpin and Fergus, who had brought the stone from Ireland, and from there, through the mists of time, to Scota and her husband Gaythelos.

Until he reached his majority at the age of twenty-one Alexander made no attempt to renew his father's efforts to annexe the Western Isles. However, in 1261 the King sent an embassy to Bergen to reopen negotiations with King Haakon. On receiving news of his emissaries' failure he decided to apply force and, in the following year, Skye was attacked by the Earl of Ross. Haakon, realising that he might have to cope with a major onslaught, collected his forces and set sail from Bergen on the 15th July 1263. He paused at Kirkwall in the Orkneys for reinforcements, which were not forthcoming, and from there his fleet of 120 ships sailed through the Sound of Skye where he was joined by Magnus, King of Man. Some forces raised in the Isles were waiting near Oban and, after Haakon's fleet joined them, they successfully attacked the castles of Rothesay in Bute and Dunaverty in Kintyre before the whole invasion force assembled in Lamlash harbour off the Isle of Arran.

Alexander had stationed most of his men at Ayr on the opposite side of the Firth of Clyde and, when Haakon arrived, the Scots made attempts to negotiate, or perhaps merely to procrastinate until summer was over and the autumn gales had set in. In late September the talks were broken off and Haakon sent off sixty ships to ravage Loch Long. His main force prepared to land at Largs and, in preparation for their arrival, Alexander's forces moved along the coast to repulse them. However on the 30th September a bad storm sprang up lasting two days and causing great damage to Haakon's fleet. Several ships ran aground and a minor battle developed when a Scottish force surprised several hundred Norwegians who were attempting to recover the cargo of a stranded merchantman. The immediate outcome of this "Battle of Largs" is not known but, although the outnumbered Norwegians made an orderly withdrawal to their ships, the Scots claimed a victory. Neither of the two kings was involved in the fighting but Haakon's nephew was reported killed. Two days later, the ships from Loch Long, also badly mauled by the gale, returned. In view of the circumstances and the worsening weather, Haakon decided to retire to Kirkwall for the winter where he could replenish supplies and repair his ships before renewing the struggle in the following spring. However, in November he fell seriously ill and in December he died. The battle of Largs was the last occasion in which Norse and Scots faced each other in armed conflict.

Haakon's failure to obtain recruits in the Orkneys, and the limited number of Islesmen who joined his expedition, must have forced the Orcadians and the Norwegians to the realisation that their hold on the Isles was no longer secure. In the spring of 1262 an embassy from Orkney arrived in Scotland but Alexander was unwilling to negotiate. During the summer he received the submission of the King of Man who made homage in order to forestall an invading army assembled in Galloway. In the same year forces were sent to Skye and the Western Isles and, in the autumn, Haakon's son, Magnus, sent ambassadors to discuss peace. Negotiations were conducted over the next two years, during which the King of Man died, and, in 1226, Magnus signed the Treaty of Perth, by which all the Western Isles were ceded to the Scots for 4000 merks and an annual payment of 100 merks in perpetuity. Alexander at last ruled the Isles and, with the exception of an expedition to Man in 1275, Scotland was at peace for the remaining twenty years of his reign.

In all his dealings with England, Alexander was careful not to compromise the independence of his kingdom. On Christmas Day, 1251, the day before his marriage to Henry's daughter, he was knighted by the English King. Following the marriage ceremony he did homage to Henry for his English lands but deftly turned aside a request to do homage for Scotland, saying that "he had come to marry and not to answer about so difficult a matter". At that time the King was only ten years old and for the next three years the country was governed by a party led by Walter Comyn, Earl of Menteith. However, a rival, pro-English group of Nobles had come into being and when squabbles broke out Henry intervened, not as a liege lord, but as a fellow monarch and the King's father-in-law. Largely by his efforts Comyn's party was forced to resign and a new administration was set up to rule for the remaining seven years of the King's minority. The new group although pro-English, obtained its strength and unity from a firm Scottish resolve to maintain stable government until the young Alexander came of age. Unfortunately it lasted only two years and, by 1256, England was of the opinion that the Scots were close to civil war. Again Henry intervened and strenuous efforts by the two kings eventually achieved a compromise between the two factions.

The question of Scottish independence was renewed at the coronation of Edward I in 1274. Alexander and his Queen both attended, but only after receiving written assurance that his position would not be compromised either by his presence or by the service, presumably the carrying of the state sword, that he was to perform. Four years later he again visited Edward's court after having requested, and received, the same written assurance. This time he paid homage for his lands in England but, strongly repudiated Edward's claim that he might also do homage for Scotland, stating quite forcefully that, "to do homage for my kingdom of Scotland no one has right except God alone, nor do I hold it except of God alone". It is, however, quite likely that Edward's claim was intended only as a future bargaining counter, because, for the remaining seven years of Alexander's reign, the two kings and their kingdoms remained on good and friendly terms.

Alexander's marriages were ill fated and the deaths of his children were to have disastrous effects on Scotland. His first wife, Margaret, died in 1275 at the comparatively early age of 35. Their oldest child, also Margaret, had been born in 1261 and was married at the age of twenty to Erik, king of Norway. Within a year she was dead leaving her husband with an infant daughter. Two boys were also born of the King's first marriage but the younger, David, died unmarried in 1281 and the elder, Alexander, died three years later without issue. At the age of 43 Scotland's King was unmarried and his only surviving heir was a young girl, not yet three years old. Edward I wrote in the most friendly terms to convey his sympathy at the tragedies which had overtaken the Royal household. But sympathy and an infant grandchild were hardly sufficient to secure the succession. Alexander must be remarried without delay and must produce more heirs. Accordingly, after the usual negotiations, he was wed to Yolande in October of 1285. Five months later, returning to his new wife after a council at Edinburgh, he became separated from his retinue after crossing the river Forth on the Queen's ferry. The guides could not find him that night but, on the following morning, he was discovered dead on the shore at Kinghorn. In the dark and storm of the previous evening his horse had slipped and carried him over the cliff.

Scotland's hopes for the future now rested with his grandchild, young Margaret, the 'Maid of Norway'. By a document signed in February 1284 the Scots nobles had agreed to recognize her as the King's rightful heir and now, following his death, six guardians were appointed to govern the kingdom during her minority. By 1290 it had been agreed that she should come to Scotland, and a marriage with Kind Edward's son, Prince Edward, had been arranged. She left Norway in September but succumbed to a short and fatal illness during the journey. Her death plunged Scotland into a disputed succession and the war of independence.

THE TURBULENT YEARS

"O Flower of Scotland,
When will we see your like again
That fought and died for
Your wee bit hill and glen?
And stood against him,
Proud Edward's army,
And sent him homeward
Tae think again."

(Words and Music: Ray Williamson,
 Arranged: The Corries
 The Corries (Music) Limited.)

THE DISPUTED SUCCESSION

Despite Alexander's apparently successful attempts to secure the nomination of his grand-daughter as heir to the Scots throne, she was not immediately recognized when he died in March of 1286. The Scots nobles had been somewhat reluctant to put their names to the document which recognized the Maid of Norway. Although unwilling to go so far as to call her their future Queen they had, failing Alexander's ability to produce a child from his second marriage, agreed that she would be their, "lady and rightful heir of our said Lord, the King of Scotland". It was possibly with some relief therefore that, when Alexander died, they were told that his widow, Queen Yolande, was carrying the King's child. No decisions could be made regarding the succession until the outcome of the Queen's pregnancy was known and the recognition of the Maid was postponed. This delay gave other claimants to the throne an opportunity to press their own claims. Robert Bruce, Lord of Annandale and grandfather of the future Robert I, opposed the right of any female to inherit the kingdom and advanced his own claim at the Scone parliament of April 1286. His ancestors had arrived in England with the Norman conquest and had later moved north in the service of David I. Bruce's father had married Isabel, second daughter of King David's grandson and this brought him into the direct line of succession. Rival claims were immediately lodged. John Balliol's forebears had also come to Scotland during King David's reign. His father had

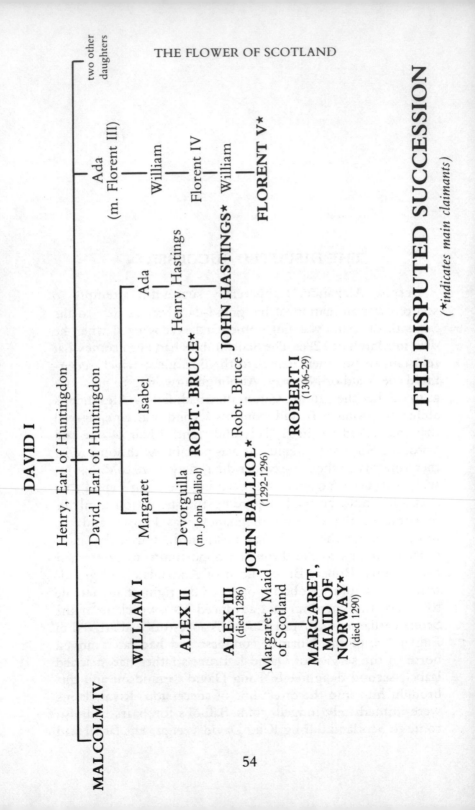

THE DISPUTED SUCCESSION

(*indicates main claimants)

married the daughter of Isabel's older sister and so, although Bruce was one generation nearer the throne, Balliol was in the senior line — he was the grandson of the eldest daughter whereas Bruce was the son of a younger daughter. In the face of these conflicting arguments, with the possibility of a post-humous heir and the previous acceptance of the Maid of Norway, Parliament temporised. Six guardians (James the Steward, William Frazer Bishop of St. Andrews, Robert Wishart Bishop of Glasgow, Duncan Earl of Fife, Alexander Comyn Earl of Buchan and John Comyn Lord of Badenoch) were appointed to govern the kingdom and to supervise the arrangements for deciding on the rightful successor. All Scots magnates swore a rather vague oath to recognise, "the nearest by blood who by right must inherit", and Parliament adjourned, leaving Scotland to the rule of the guardians.

By the end of the year it became apparent that Yolande had either miscarried or had been feigning pregnancy. Bruce and Balliol seemed ready to use force to make good their claims on the throne and, in the winter months, conditions deteriorated to the extent that the host had to be called out to uphold the law. Throughout the next two years Scotland hovered on the brink of civil war and no solution to the problems of succession appeared in sight. Then, in April 1289, a Norwegian embassy arrived in England with a proposal that the Maid of Norway be married to King Edward's son and heir. Edward now asked the guardians to meet the Norwegians and discuss the position of the Maid. The outcome of the negotiations was the Treaty of Salisbury by which Margaret, Maid of Norway, was formally recognized as heir to the Scots throne. She was to be sent to Scotland, or England, before November 1290 and entrusted to the care of Edward who would deliver her, unmarried and with no marital agreements, as soon as Scotland was stable and at peace. By March 1290, when the treaty was ratified, rumours of an engagement with Edward's son were beginning to circulate. The Scots reacted with pleasure at the prospects of such a match — Alexander himself had once hinted at its desirability — and a marriage treaty was negotiated at

Birgham in July. Although the proposed union was joyfully accepted, care was taken to ensure that Scotland would remain "separate and divided from England, according to its rightful boundaries". Scots customs, liberties, and laws were to continue as before and the country was to be "free in itself and without subjection". The English agreed but the safeguards were nullified to some extent by a clause stipulating that agreement was made "saving the right of our said Lord Edward". The inclusion of such a statement was fairly standard practice, but during the reign of the late Alexander, Edward had twice suggested that homage was due to him as the overlord of Scotland and, in effect, the clause meant that he had not given up this claim.

The effects of Edward's influence had begun to creep into Scottish affairs even before the marriage treaty was signed. Following Alexander's death in 1286 Scottish envoys visited Edward and may have requested his aid in resolving the disputes. At that time there was little indication of the troubles which were to follow. Edward had obtained a reputation as a successful mediator in continental disputes and Scotland and England had been at peace for many years. His sister had been married to the late Alexander and it must have seemed natural to turn to this elder statesman for advice. However, Edward had never given up his hope that the two countries would be eventually merged and, to the concern of the Scots, he began to take an active interest in Scottish affairs. These concerns were most prevalent among the clergy who jealously guarded the independence of the kirk and worried that this might slip away. In matters of both church and state the situation appeared somewhat ominous. When Pope Gregory levied a tax on clerical income to finance a new crusade the Scots clergy were ordered to pay the tax to Edward. Foreign creditors of Alexander III raised court actions in England to recover their debts and Edward had assumed control of the Isle of Man. With the ratification of the marriage treaty he was in a position to act more decisively. The Bishop of Durham was appointed to be the Scottish agent of the young couple and Edward, on the basis of preserving law and order on behalf of the future monarch, ordered the guardians to obey the Bishop in all matters. "On account of certain dangers and suspicions", he demanded the keys to Scotland's castles and it was all the Guardians could do to temporise until the Maid sailed from Norway. Her death in September, while en route to Scotland brought the possibility of a peaceful and orderly transition to an end. Bruce and Balliol began to gather their followers and, in early October, Bishop Frazer, one of the four remaining Guardians, sent England news of Bruce's aggressive actions with a suggestion that Edward intervene on behalf of John Balliol to prevent Civil War. The following month Balliol issued a charter styling himself as "heir to the Kingdom of Scotland". Bruce countered these moves by placing himself under the protection of Edward and making a formal protest, in the name of the seven Earls of Scotland, against any of the Guardians acting independently.

With the situation in Scotland now rapidly deteriorating, Edward moved to assume control. Early in the following year he gathered together all records pertaining to his right as overlord of Scotland, arranged for the provision of English ships which might be useful in a blockade, sent 10,000 merks to Newcastle — for use in war or diplomacy as required — and summoned an army to Norham castle on the English side of the Tweed. In May of 1291 he arrived at Norham and announced to the Scots that he had come, "to do justice to everyone as sovereign", with the explanation that his moves were justified "by virtue of the overlordship", that belonged to him. When he requested the Scots to formally accept his claim, the deputation which had met him at Norham made the mistake of replying that only the King of Scotland could recognize him as overlord and that, because they had no king, they could not "make answer". They no doubt thought that their answer had successfully avoided this dangerous issue but Edward, who had perhaps been ready for this type of answer, now put the question to each of the competitors. By then Bruce and Balliol had been joined by seven other claimants and each in turn, and with probable hopes for the crown, agreed to accept Edward's claim. As one of these would, in due course, become the rightful King of Scots, the previous evasion had been successfully countered and at last Edward had the acknowledgement that he so dearly desired. As the now acknowledged overlord of Scotland, Edward was free to exert his authority. Scots castles were handed over to the English and Edward rode through the country to obtain oaths of fealty before opening the first session of "The Great Cause" at Berwick on 2 August 1291.

The purpose of the Great Cause was to determine which of the rival claimants would be king. By the time the courts sat the ranks of the hopeful had swelled. There were now twelve competitors but only four had really significant claims. These were John Balliol, Robert Bruce, John Hastings and Count Florent IV of Holland. The first three traced their descent from the daughters of King David's grandson. Balliol was the grandson of the eldest daughter. Bruce, now an octogenarian, was the son of the second daughter and Hastings was the grandson of the youngest. Bruce and Balliol both lodged a claim for the throne itself but Hastings, perhaps realising that he had little hope of success, attempted to have the Kingdom partitioned among the three. This was the common practice in baronies when there were only daughters to inherit but Bruce disputed these arguments and asserted that a kingdom was indivisible. Unlike the other three, Florent was descended, not from a grandson, but from a younger grand-daughter of David I. Under normal circumstances his claim would have been immediately disallowed but he declared that the grandson (David Earl of Huntingdon), from whom the other three traced their lineage, had voluntarily surrendered his right to the throne. He also stated that William IV had stipulated that, if his own line should fail (as it did when Alexander III died), the throne should pass to the descendants of his younger sister Ada, the great, great, grandmother of Florent. The Count also claimed that written evidence existed in the Scottish records to prove the truth of his statements.

After listening to Florent the court adjourned to provide

him with time to uncover the evidence in support of his claim. However, when it reopened on 2 June 1292 another claimant presented himself. Erik of Norway joined the competitors with the rather spurious claim that, if his daughter the Maid of Norway, had previously been judged to be the rightful heir, then he, as her father, must now have the best claim. The court now had to deal with thirteen claims and counter claims and, in an attempt to bring order to the hearings decided to proceed firstly with those which were the most obvious and best substantiated. Accordingly it was agreed that, without prejudice to any others, the court would first settle the rival claims of John Balliol and Robert Bruce.

By 6th November Edward's lawyers had decided in favour of Balliol and Bruce, having lost the case, transferred his claim to his descendants. The remaining competitors were speedily dealt with. Hasting's submission that the kingdom was divisible was decided to be unlawful. Florent's claim failed because he was unable to support his case with substantive evidence and six of the other candidates withdrew from the proceedings. The two remaining claimants, John Comyn and Erik of Norway, did not press their claims which then lapsed. Indeed, it is probable that Erik had only entered the case to obtain bargaining power in other matters he wished to settle. Comyn, being married to Balliol's sister, no doubt appreciated the position he would hold as the King's brother-in-law and did not wish to compromise his power by opposition at this late stage.

On the 17th November 1292, Edward handed down a formal judgment in favour of John Balliol. He was crowned at Scone on St. Andrew's Day and joined his overlord at Newcastle for Christmas. There he did homage and was warned to rule justly and wisely so that Edward would have no cause to interfere directly in Scottish affairs.

John Balliol (Toom Tabard)
Born c 1250
Reigned: 1292-1296
Son of Devorguilla, great, great, grand-daughter of David I
Married daughter of Earl of Surrey
Two sons
Contemporary of Edward I (Hammer of the Scots) 1272-1307
Died and buried in Picardy, France.

John Balliol, whose ancestors had held land in England under William Rufus and moved to Scotland in the time of David I, was pronounced King of Scots on the 17th November 1292 and was crowned at Scone on 30th November. He had only recently inherited the Lordship of Galloway and, prior to lodging his claim to the throne, his interests had been centred more in France and England than in Scotland. Holding land and manors in seventeen English shires, he was essentially an Anglo-Norman and became elevated to the throne through the relationship of his mother to King David I.

Edward I, King of England, had been requested to adjudicate the disputes which arose when the House of Canmore failed on the death of Alexander III. He agreed to do so after the Scots had accepted him as overlord and Balliol was thus a vassal King. However, this did not mean that he could not rule effectively in Scotland. In his first parliament, held in February 1293, he attempted to continue the consolidation of the North and West which had been so ably begun by the Alexanders. Three new sheriffdoms were created; in Kintyre, Lorne and Skye. Royal authority had lapsed during the six years in which Scotland had lacked a king. John attempted to restore the power of the crown but was overtaken by events.

The trouble started in the courts. When Edward was accepted as overlord, he automatically became the highest legal authority in the country and appeals could now be made to him against rulings of the high court of Scotland. However, when the marriage treaty of 1290 had been signed,

Scotland had been guaranteed its independence in matters of law and the Scots who had accepted Edward no doubt hoped that he would not exercise his new powers to the full. In this they were to be disappointed. Edward refused to give up his right to hear appeals in England and King John was placed in the humiliating position of having to agree that Edward was not bound by any promises made to the Scots before he was acknowledged as their overlord.

At first John attempted to avoid the consequences of this agreement and simply ignored the appeals which began to appear. However this was unsatisfactory because the King of Scots, or a Scots deputation, were certainly required at the appeal court to defend and explain the decisions against which an appeal was made. In an attempt to finally settle the matter Edward's council forced the issue with a ruling that, in all such cases the King of Scots must appear in person before the appeal court. In 1293 King John did, at last, attend an appeal but announced that "he could not discuss anything touching his kingdom without the advice of his people". The court offered to adjourn so that this advice could be obtained but this was refused because to accept an adjournment would have been tantamount to acknowledging English supremacy in legal matters. As a result John was declared to be in contempt of court and was ordered to bind over various Scottish castles and towns as a penalty for defying his liegelord. The only alternatives were to submit or to risk all out war. John reluctantly chose the former and accepted Edward's jurisdiction over the Scots High Court. By themselves these decisions would have been sufficient to cause concern over the new order of things but the problems were compounded by what was perceived as quite unwarranted interference in internal Scottish affairs. Through the period when the 'great cause' was being heard, Edward had governed Scotland in person and there was naturally some unfinished business when the crown was settled on John Balliol. Instead of leaving the new king to finish off these matters Edward decided to attend to them in person and the Scots felt increasingly threatened as they saw the independence of their country slip away. Dissatisfaction spread and matters were brought to a head with the outbreak of an English-French war. Edward ordered his vassal Scots to provide men and arms to aid him in the coming struggle but, although John was forced to promise assistance, the Scots magnates had no wish to become involved in England's foreign wars. In the summer of 1295, within a year of John's promise of help, a Scots embassy was sent to France to conclude an alliance of mutual aid against the common enemy. Scotland and England prepared for war which erupted in March of the following year when Edward took Berwick amid great slaughter. The Earls of Ross, Menteith and Athol retaliated by leading their men on large scale raids in Tynedale and Redesdale but, within a month, the fighting was brought to a bloody conclusion by the superior English army. On the 27th April the Scots were trounced at Dunbar. Their castles fell to Edward soon after and all resistance vanished. Without an army there seemed no possibility of continuing the struggle and in July King John surrendered at Kincardine. He acknowledged his errors in opposing his overlord and, after resigning the kingdom into Edward's hands, was formally stripped of the regal regalia, a ceremony which gave him his nickname 'Toom Tabard' (empty coat).

Edward toured Scotland to ensure that no pockets of resistance held out against him and, with their king gone, the Scots leaders hastily renounced the Franco-Scottish alliance and submitted to Edward. Thirty-five parchments — the Ragman Rolls — were required to contain the names of those who swore fealty to Edward during his journey. John was held captive in England for the next three years before being permitted to retire, in exile, to his French estates. Thereafter he took no part in the affairs of his former kingdom and died, aged 63, in 1313.

THE WAR OF INDEPENDENCE

Realising that the revolt which had just been put down had originated not with John Balliol but with the leading Scottish nobles, Edward made no arrangements to crown a new, vassal, King of Scots. Instead he decided to rule directly from London. The Scottish regalia and the stone of Scone were removed to Westminster and in future he was to refer to "the land of Scotland" rather than to "the kingdom". By October of 1296 the Scots Kirk, the last distinctly Scottish institution, had begun to be infiltrated with English clerics and within a year of Balliol's defeat Edward was to rule that all vacant positions in the Scots Kirk were to be filled with Englishmen.

It became increasingly obvious that, if Edwards's plans were carried through to their logical conclusions, Scotland would cease to exist as a separate entity and would become little more than a northern extension of England. There was little that the Scots lords could do because most had bound themselves to Edward by oaths of loyalty made after the defeat at Dunbar. However, the church had been less eager to give up its independence. Only three of the Scots Bishops had done homage to the English King and one of these, the Bishop of Glasgow, now began to secretly encourage and foment another rising. Resistance began in a small way with scattered outbreaks of fighting in various parts of the country. William Wallace, the second son of a lesser Renfrewshire knight, had not taken part in the humiliating submission of the Scots nobility and became involved in a fracas at Lanark, possibly because of his failure to submit. He escaped from Edward's men with the aid of his wife but, on learning that she had been killed in the fighting, Wallace immediately returned to seek revenge. He hunted out the English Sheriff, killed him, and fled from the town, an outlaw with a price on his head. Around him Wallace gathered a motley force of commoners and in May joined forces with Sir William Douglas. Together they descended on Scone where William Ormsby, Edward's justiciar, was holding his court. Ormsby's defeat and flight was the signal for the scattered outbreaks of resistance to assume the proportions of open rebellion. Bishop Wishart and the Steward of Scotland now openly joined the rebels. Robert

Bruce, grandson of the competitor and now Earl of Carrick, also joined forces but it is suspected that his motives were not of the purest. Wallace and the others were fighting in the name of John Balliol with the avowed intention of restoring their deposed King and it appears likely that Bruce was more interested in asserting his own claim to the throne. This division within the Scottish ranks was to have grave results. On 7th July the Scots force came face to face with English troops at Irvine and, before battle was joined, a Scots knight changed sides declaring that it was foolish to fight in an army which had no common purpose. The resolve to continue the struggle dissolved and most of the other nobles, including Bruce, Wishart and the Steward, withdrew to the English ranks. With the departure of these 'natural' leaders the battle was avoided. Edward offered lenient terms of submission to those who had gone over to the English and the rebellion appeared to have fizzled out before it had really started. At the end of August Edward left England for Flanders, convinced that his problems with the rebellious Scots were largely over.

However the submission at Irvine merely served to change the leadership of the Scots resistance and did not eliminate the basic will to resist. With the Scots lords utterly discredited in the eyes of the common people, Wallace emerged as a guerilla leader in his own right. After Irvine he took his small army of commoners north to join the rebels led by Andrew Moray, heir to large estates in Moray and the Black Isle. For generations the province of Moray had been a hotbed of dissent and the scattered risings which had taken place there had gone from strength to strength. The North began to slip from English control and Hugh Cressingham, Edward's treasurer, and the Earl of Surrey were sent to deal with the rebels. Their army of 10,000 foot soldiers and 300 knights on horseback met the combined forces of Wallace and Moray on September 11th at Stirling.

The two armies were separated by the River Forth. The Scots were on the north bank and the English on the south. After a few false starts Cressingham's men began to cross the narrow wooden bridge which provided the only route over the river. Wallace waited until they were partly across and then swept down to achieve the first major Scottish victory for many years. The English were totally vanquished and chased from the field. Cressingham was killed during the battle and, when his body was found, it was skinned to provide souveniers for the victorious Scots. Within a few months Moray died from wounds sustained during the battle and Wallace became the undisputed leader of Scotland. He was knighted and proclaimed the sole Guardian but, still fighting for his exiled King, he styled himself, "William Wallace, Knight, Guardian of the Kingdom of Scotland and commander of its armies in the name of the famous prince, the Lord John, by God's grace the illustrious King of Scotland, by the consent of the community of that realm".

After the battle of 'Stirling brig', Scotland fell almost totally from English control and Wallace was able to carry the war into the enemy's camp. Berwick was soon recovered and, in November while famine raged at home, Wallace invaded the north of England. However in March of the following year Edward returned from Flanders and immediately began to prepare an attack on his rebellious subjects. By July he had advanced to Roxburgh and set out for Edinburgh where he had arranged to contact ships dispatched with food for his troops. On his arrival at Edinburgh he learned that bad weather had prevented most of the fleet from reaching the Forth. Those which had made a safe landing carried little food and were stocked mostly with wine. Supplies quickly ran short and, with many of his troops either starving or drunk, Edward was close to retreat when news was brought that Wallace was at Falkirk, only a few miles away. Thoughts of retreat vanished with the prospects of fighting a conclusive action and battle was joined on 22nd July 1298. Falkirk was a disaster for Wallace. His army was cut to pieces, partly because of the lack of heavy cavalry, and the Scots were slaughtered. Wallace escaped from the field but the punishing defeat made it impossible to maintain his position as leader and he resigned the guardianship on the banks of the Forth. Nevertheless the example he had set over the last year was not ignored. As Edward set about restoring his power in Scotland new leaders emerged. Initially Robert Bruce and John Comyn, son of Balliol's sister, acted as Guardians in the name of King John. But the uneasy alliance between these two could not last. In August of 1299 the Bishop of Glasgow emerged as the chief Guardian and, within a short time, Bruce had been replaced by a Knight whose loyalty to Balliol was unquestioned.

Edward established his rule over Southern Scotland in the summer of 1300 with an expedition to Galloway and was quartered there when a Papal Bull arrived. In it Pope Boniface stated that, "the kingdom of Scotland pertained . . . to the Roman Church and that, as we understood, it was not feudally subject to your ancestors . . . nor is it so to you". Edward was required to present evidence to the Papal Court justifying his claim to overlordship and, during a truce arranged through the intervention of France, the reply was prepared. The Guardians also sent envoys to Rome in order to rebut English claims and discussions dragged on until May 1301 when the truce expired. Over the next two years there was sporadic but inconclusive warfare. Edward had achieved control over most of Southern Scotland but the Guardians were entrenched North of the Forth and could not be shifted. Bruce, perhaps in pique, took little or no part in the fighting and indeed had submitted to Edward and, "yielded himself to the peace of the King". The respite from all out war worked to the advantage of the English. Between 1301 and 1303 Edward reached a settlement in his disputes with France and so became free to deal with Scotland without constantly looking over his shoulder for possible trouble on the continent. His negotiations with the Pope were also resolved when the Papal Court became persuaded that his claims were justified and wrote to the Scots Bishops blaming the war on their intransigence.

Realising that the war could only be won by striking at the Scottish heartland north of the Forth, Edward made plans to cross the river. In May of 1303 he set out from Roxburgh with 7000 men in a carefully timed march which ended at the Forth within a few days of the arrival of floating bridges towed up the coast from Lynn. Quickly over the river he was in Perth by June and on the Moray Firth by September. His rapid movements once again broke the back of Scottish resistance and the north was quickly subdued. Retiring to Dunfermline, where he set up his headquarters, Edward again offered lenient terms to those who were prepared to surrender. As in the past most of the nobles hurried to his call. No terms were offered to Wallace however who had been brought back into the Scottish ranks in a subservient role. He was specifically excluded from Edward's offer of peace and fought his last skirmish in September of 1304. Thereafter, with most of the country in English hands, he lived the life of a hunted outlaw. Betrayed and captured in August of the following year he was taken to Westminster and judged guilty of treason. At Smithfield he suffered the fate which had been specially devised for traitors. Strung up on a gallows until half dead he was brought down and disembowelled before he expired.

Once again Edward had achieved complete and utter victory. With the execution of Wallace all resistance seemed at an end and, realising that Scotland could not be held by force alone, Edward attempted to pacify the nobles. Forfeited lands were returned to them and arrangements were made to give the Scots some say in the government of their land. Once again Edward decided against replacing Balliol. Instead Scotland was to be governed by an administration comprising twenty-one Englishmen, nominated by the King, and ten Scots, selected to represent the nobility.

Robert Bruce had taken no part in the recent rebellion and was no doubt hoping that Edward's success would lead to a reconsideration of his own claim to the throne. However, when it became apparent that matters were proceeding along entirely different lines Bruce entered a pact with the Bishop of St. Andrews and secretly began to look for support. He approached John 'the Red' Comyn who embodied the Balliol cause and the original Comyn claim of 1291. The two met in Greyfriars Kirk at Dumfries on 10th February 1306. Discussions led to an argument. Tempers rose and in the heat of the moment Bruce stabbed and wounded Comyn who was then killed by one of Bruce's followers. Guilty of murder, sacrilege and, now obviously, treason Bruce could only survive by seizing power and renewing the struggle. Moving quickly he crossed the Forth with only sixty armed supporters and, on 25th March, was installed at Scone by Isabel, the Countess of Buchan.

Robert I (The Bruce)

Born 1274
Reigned 1306-1329
Son of Robert Bruce, Earl of Carrick, and grandson of Bruce 'the Competitor'
Married:
(1) Isabella, daughter of Earl of Mar
(2) Elizabeth, daughter of Earl of Ulster
One daughter by Isabella
Two sons (one died in infancy) and two daughters by Elizabeth
Contemporary of:
Edward I (the Hammer of the Scots) 1272-1307
Edward II 1307-1327
Edward III 1327-1377
Died at Cardross
Buried at Dunfermline — heart interred at Melrose

The Bruce family's claim to the throne originated with Robert's grandfather, the competitor, who was descended from David I. When Balliol was judged to be the rightful heir to the Kingdom the ageing competitor transferred his claim to his son and grandson, then only seventeen years old. After Balliol's fall from grace the Bruce actions varied among neutrality, support for Scotland and submission to Edward. They seem to have acted continually with an eye on the crown, taking part in the rebellion when it suited them but

ROBERT I (THE BRUCE)
1306-1329

daughter by Isab.   son by Eliz.

Marjorie m. Walter the Steward   **DAVID II**
                                                   1329-71

ROBERT II
1371-90

ROBERT III
1390-1406

JAMES I

BRUCE AND THE EARLY
STEWARTS

quickly changing sides to ensure that if Edward crushed the opposition their claim would receive his kindly consideration. Little support was given to the armies fighting in the name of King John and only after the murder of Comyn did Bruce make an open and determined bid for power.

When he seized the throne in 1306 Robert's position was most insecure. Not only was most of Scotland in English hands but, by his murder of John Comyn, Bruce had initiated a blood feud with one of the most powerful Scottish families. Once again, however, the Kirk rose to the occasion and provided the backbone of support for the new leader. The Bishop of St. Andrews was brought, somewhat unwillingly, to Scone to celebrate mass in honour of the new King. Bishop Wishart, of Glasgow, absolved him of his sins and, throughout the country, sermons were preached in his favour. Recruits flocked to the Bruce standard. Many came from the ancestral lands of Annandale and Carrick but, although the commoners were eager to serve this successor to Wallace, little support was obtained from the estranged nobles.

The initial year of Bruce's campaign was an unmitigated disaster. In June he was vanquished by an English force at Perth and lost many of his supporters by capture or desertion. Shortly afterwards a Scots force led by relatives of John Comyn defeated him at Dalry. In September most of his family were captured. His wife, Elizabeth was restricted to a gloomy manor house and his sisters were imprisoned, one in a nunnery and the other in a latticework cage perched high on the walls of Roxburgh castle. Cages were also prepared at Berwick castle for the Countess of Buchan and at the Tower of London for his daughter. The Countess was not released from her confinement until June of 1310, but Edward revoked the punishment designed for Bruce's daughter, perhaps because of her youth, and she was sent to a nunnery in Yorkshire.

After his flight from Dalry Bruce disappeared from sight until the end of the year. Most probably he hid in the North and West and there are convincing arguments to indicate that he obtained sanctuary in the Orkneys. Legend suggests that he was close to throwing up the struggle during these months but decided to renew his efforts after watching the fabled spider "try, try and try again". At the end of January 1307 reports that he was in the Southern Hebrides reached Edward on his sick bed at Lannercost. Ships were sent to intercept him but Bruce managed to evade his pursuers and re-appeared in the West to attack the English at Turnberry. Again he met with a personal reverse. Although the attack at Turnberry was successful a complementary raid on Loch Ryan by his brothers, Alexander and Thomas, met with defeat at the hands of a Scots family attached to the Comyns. The two brothers were captured and immediately sent south to Edward who arranged for their speedy execution.

With little or nothing yet achieved Bruce resorted to guerilla tactics, avoiding large scale battles, but forever exerting pressure and attacking small detachments when he could be sure of success. In May of 1307 a more important engagement was fought and won at Loudoun Hill in Ayrshire. Less than two months later the whole situation changed when Edward I died in the midst of preparations to bring an army over the Solway. There can be little doubt that his death was the single most important factor leading to Bruce's eventual triumph. The new king of England, Edward II, lacked both the purpose and ability to press the war with the success his father had achieved, and Bruce was given time to overcome the Scottish resistance to his rule. Free of the fear of a superior English army he turned his attention to the Comyns and those who still wished for the return of Balliol. Their strongholds lay in Galloway, Argyll and the North East and it was there that Bruce attacked them. In September Galloway was forced into making payments for a short truce. In November Inverlochy fell and the Earl of Ross paid for a truce extended to Caithness, Sutherland and Ross. Castles at Nairn and Inverness were reduced by fire and Elgin was besieged. In the spring of the following year the power of the Comyns was totally destroyed by a victory at Inverurie and the devastation of the

Comyn lands in Buchan. Aberdeen was taken in the summer of 1308 and Galloway was brought into submission by the efforts of Edward Bruce and James Douglas. The Lord of Argyll submitted at the end of the year but later resisted only to be conclusively defeated in the Pass of Brander.

By the end of 1309 Bruce had effectively disposed of the Scottish opposition and was master of two thirds of Scotland. English and Anglo-Scottish garrisons held out in the South but in the North only Perth, Dundee and Banff remained under their control. The Civil War had been won and, as things began to return to normal, trade with the continent increased. Indeed the country was sufficiently stable during 1309 for a parliament to be held at St. Andrews where the opportunity was taken to proclaim Bruce's acceptance by the people of Scotland and to declare his regality to the world at large. In the summer of 1310 Edward set out from Berwick in a long delayed attempt to recover the regions which had fallen from English control. He found that Bruce was not to be enticed into a major engagement and, after marching to and fro in vain attempts to find the Scottish army he retired in frustration to Berwick in December. There he remained for six months before returning to England to deal with internal problems caused by the English lords' opposition to his friend and advisor, Piers Gaveston.

In the autumn of 1311 Bruce invaded the North of England and obtained the funds necessary to renew his efforts to expel the remaining English forces. Cattle in their hundreds were driven over the border into Scotland and the sum of £2000, comparable to the entire Scottish revenue, was extracted from Northumberland. Dundee was taken in the spring of 1312 and Perth succumbed to a winter siege. The last strongholds in the South West fell soon after and Bruce sailed to regain the Isle of Man, leaving his brother Edward to deal with Stirling castle which still held out against him. The castle's commander offered to surrender if no reinforcements had arrived from England by midsummer's day and, rather than carry out a protracted siege, Edward Bruce accepted the suggestion. With the situation at Stirling under control the Scots set out to regain the South East and attacked in Lothian where a dozen castles were still held by the English and Anglo-Scots. Linlithgow, Roxburgh and Edinburgh fell over the year but appeals to Edward and the expiring truce at Stirling roused the English King to action. Having apparently reached a settlement with the barons Edward assembled his army and left Berwick in June of 1314. With him marched between 15,000 and 17,000 infantry supported by more than 2000 armoured knights. By the 23rd of the month he was within three miles of Stirling castle and had technically raised the siege. However between five and ten thousand Scots, led by their King in person, lay between him and the castle, and the opportunity to force a battle seemed too good to lose. Bruce had almost decided to retire from the field. On other occasions he had slipped away when confronted by superior odds, but a defector to the Scots army gave him important news. English morale was low and their troops had taken up a poor position on marshy ground, hemmed in between the River Forth and the Bannock Burn. With the Scots entrenched on high ground, and surrounded by trees to provide cover from archers and cavalry, Bruce decided to fight.

As day dawned on the 24th June, four massive Scottish infantry battalions pushed down the hill with their long spears at the ready. In their confined position between the two rivers the English had little room for manoeuvre and were pressed back against the Bannock Burn. Men at the rear began to retreat but found it difficult to cross to the other side. Many slipped or fell and the resulting confusion turned the retreat into a rout. Bruce's infantry and camp followers fell on the stricken English army which was totally defeated and put to flight. King Edward, with some of his cavalry, escaped to the castle but the commander had decided to surrender to Bruce and the King was forced to retire in haste.

The immediate effect of Bannockburn was the recovery of all Scotland, except Berwick, from the English and Anglo-Scots. Prisoners were exchanged and Robert welcomed back his wife, sister, daughter and nephew. But if the Scots hoped for peace they were disappointed. Edward made no moves to indicate that he was willing to come to terms. In an attempt to weld the Scots firmly together, Bruce held a Parliament at Cambuskenneth, near Stirling, in November 1314 and disinherited all those who had opposed him. No longer would a Scot be able to hold land in both countries and be a subject of both Kings. The following year his brother Edward Bruce, who had fought so well in the war against England, was declared his heir and the succession seemed well secured.

Within a year the war of attrition was resumed. Bruce initiated raids in the north of England partly to raise funds for the coming struggle but also to lower English morale in an attempt to force Edward to sue for peace. At the same time a second front was opened in Ireland to deprive the English of troops and provisions. Edward Bruce sailed from Scotland to lead the new campaign and was proclaimed high king of Ireland in 1316. For two years he created havoc among the English and Anglo-Irish but Bruce's long term plans of a loose union of Ireland and Scotland came to nothing. In 1318 the Scottish expeditionary force was decisively beaten and Scotland lost its heir when Edward Bruce was killed. The Irish campaign did not, however, divert Bruce from action at home. Raids in northern England were frequent and, in March of 1318, Berwick itself fell. When Edward attempted to retake the town by siege in the following year, Bruce counter-attacked with an invasion of England which forced Edward to withdraw. The war had reached a stalemate. Edward was unable to gain control in any part of Scotland but Bruce was equally unable to force him to accept peace terms or to recognise Scotland as an independent kingdom. A two year truce was agreed on the 22nd December 1319.

Almost two years previously the Pope had placed Scotland under interdict and excommunicated Bruce because of the protracted fighting. Scotland now attempted to justify the war. In spring 1320 the Declaration of Arbroath was drawn up and sent to Rome. The document drew attention to the protection Scotland had received from other Popes in previous years and maintained that the land had always been an independent kingdom until Edward I had attempted to deprive the Scots of their independence. It stated that King Robert had been chosen as the rightful King and strongly asserted the Scots determination to resist subjection to England; "for so long as a hundred men remain alive we will never in any way be bowed beneath the yoke of English domination". The Pope was by no means convinced by the arguments put forward and merely urged the two countries to make peace. Negotiations were indeed held in January and April of 1321 but these proved quite fruitless and, on the expiry of the truce in January the following year, Bruce renewed the raids on England. In May Edward prepared for another invasion and marched to Edinburgh to meet English ships which had sailed in advance. Bruce reverted to his original policy of avoiding a major engagement and instead deprived the invading army of fodder and provisions by laying waste to the countryside in their path. When Edward reached Edinburgh he found that his supply ships had been held back by foul weather in the North Sea. Unlike Wallace, Bruce was not to be enticed into battle on Scottish soil and, with his supplies running low, Edward was forced into an ignominious retreat. Bruce crossed the border in pursuit and put the English to flight at a battle near Byland Abbey. Again a stalemate was reached. Despite the victory at Byland, Bruce was in no position to follow up his success by penetrating deep into England. Another truce was arranged. This one was intended to last for thirteen years and, although it broke down after only four, it provided the Scots with their first real respite from the war which had been conducted almost incessantly for the last sixteen years.

War had changed Scotland in many ways. Large areas of the countryside had become depopulated and rural life had suffered considerably. The productivity of the land had fallen by nearly half and arable farming in the south had been largely abandoned to raise sheep and cattle which could more easily be moved out of the way of marauding troops. More wool was now available for export. Trade was encouraged and burghs assumed greater importance than they had in the past. Bruce increased the number of baronies and more control was given to local governments. Castles were erected or repaired and, during the general reconstruction, a manor house was built at Cardross for the exclusive use of the King. An heir, David, was born in the second year of the truce and the safe descent of the crown was secured when Robert Stewart, the young son of Marjory Bruce and already named as successor if Bruce died without male issue, was named to succeed him if David failed to produce heirs of his own.

Peace talks were held in the winter of 1324 but Edward still refused to acknowledge Bruce as the King of an independent country. Although Edward abided carefully by the conditions of the truce he was unable, or unwilling, to control English privateers who preyed on Scots ships travelling to and from the Continent. The fragile truce began to fall apart. A Franco-Scottish alliance was concluded in 1326 and cultural ties developed with France to replace those which had once existed with England. Conditions in England had also changed. Edward II was deposed by his Queen and her lover Roger Mortimer who began to rule in the name of the young prince, now proclaimed Edward III. Bruce marked the day of his coronation (February 1327) with a raid on Norham Castle and at Easter sailed to Ulster to stir up revolt. By July Ulster had been forced to conclude a truce and King Robert returned to Scotland while his nobles invaded the north of England. Isabella and Mortimer hastened to defend their northern domains but were put to flight in a night attack. The Scots army retired over the border and the English retreated to disband at York. However no sooner had their army dispersed than Bruce gathered fresh troops and advanced with the stated intention of annexing Northumberland. Mortimer and Isabella could not raise another army at such short notice and were forced to sue for peace.

The peace treaty gave Bruce everything he had fought for. Edward III admitted that he and his predecessors had caused the war by wrongfully claiming the overlordship of Scotland. Scotland was at last acknowledged as an independent and sovereign kingdom ruled by, "that magnificent prince, the Lord Robert by the grace of God, King of Scots, our ally and dear friend". The boundary between the two countries was fixed as it had been when Alexander III died and a pact of mutual aid was concluded in so far as it did not contravene the earlier Franco-Scottish alliance. The treaty was ratified at Holyrood on 17th March 1328 and at Northampton on the 4th of May. In July the new 'friendship' was cemented by a royal marriage between Edward's sister Joan and the young prince David. Edward interceded with the Pope on Scotland's behalf. The interdict was lifted and Bruce was welcomed back into the arms of the church.

By now, however, Bruce was ill and near to his end. After a last visit to Ulster and a tiring pilgrimage to the Shrine of St. Ninian at Whithorn he retired to his manor at Cardross. There, with the loyal Lords of Scotland in attendance, he died on 7th June 1329. Before his death he told them of his long cherished ambition to fight on a crusade and requested the Lord Douglas to carry his heart to the Holy Land. The King's last wish was partly fulfilled. Following the funeral ceremony at Dunfermline Douglas took his heart "against the enemies of God". He journeyed to Flanders and then to Spain where he fought in a Christian army against the Moors. Although Douglas was killed in battle, the heart of Bruce was brought home to be interred at Melrose.

David II
Born 1324
Reigned: 1329-1371
Son of Robert I
Contemporary of Edward III 1327-1377
Married:
(1) Joan, sister of Edward III
(2) Margaret Drummond, widow of Sir John Logie
No children
Died at Edinburgh

When Robert the Bruce died, Scotland could seemingly look forward to years of increasing prosperity. The ruinous wars with England had been brought to a triumphant conclusion. Scotland's independence had been recognised and a peace treaty, guaranteeing freedom from English domination, had been enhanced by the marriage of the young David to Edward III's sister Joan. For two years all went smoothly but Bruce's overwhelming success and his resistance to any form of compromise contained the seeds of future problems. David was installed at the end of 1331 and, for the first time, the new monarch was anointed and crowned with all the solemnity of the Catholic church. At his coronation David was only seven years old and, by a settlement made in 1315, Thomas Randolph, the Earl of Moray, was appointed to act as Regent. Moray had been a close friend of Robert I. He had led the left wing of the Scottish troops at Bannockburn and there was every reason to believe that Scotland would thrive under his strong leadership. However, events soon took a different course.

When the peace treaty of 1328 had been signed, no mention was made of the disinherited Scots lords who had fought against Bruce and had allied themselves to the Comyn-Balliol faction. Edward's Queen, Isabella, attempted to procure the return of their lands when she visited Scotland for the Royal wedding with the suggestion that the Scottish regalia and the Stone of Scone might be returned from Westminster. Her efforts were largely ignored. Certainly,

Moray did indeed reinstate some of the disinherited but he would not consider the return of land to those who were firmly opposed to the new order. In England Edward III seized power from his mother, Isabella and her paramour, Mortimer, and began to rule with the strength and clarity of his grandfather, 'the hammer of the Scots'. He backed the nobles' demands to be reinstated and when it became clear that his political efforts were to no avail the disinherited decided to use force in an attempt to overthrow David and Moray. Their leader, Henry Beaumout, heir to the vast lands of Buchan, invited Edward Balliol, son of the late King John, to join them in a bid for the throne. In the summer of 1332 their preparations were well in hand and Moray was preparing to receive them when he died mysteriously in June. Poison was suspected but no proof was ever shown. Balliol and Beaumont sailed with their troops at the end of July and, while they were at sea, the Scots hurriedly chose a new Regent, the Earl of Mar, cousin to the young King. Balliol's troops landed at Kinghorn on the 6th August. They were resisted by the Earl of Fife but appeared to have had little difficulty in pushing him aside and continuing their march. As they proceeded inland they were opposed by the main Scottish force under the Earl of Mar. The two armies met on Dupplin Moor near Perth and it was immediately seen that the Scots had the superiority in both numbers and position. As a result they were careless. Pickets were not posted properly, many of the men got drunk and on the morning of the 11th August they woke up to find that the situation had completely changed. During the night Balliol's men had moved and they were now in a strong defensive position. The Scots attacked and the English archers took their toll. By the end of the day the English were in full control of the battle field. The Regent Mar was killed and the Scots were massacred. Perth fell almost immediately and on the 24th September, Balliol was crowned King of Scots.

Edward had not officially supported Balliol but he now called a council and argued that Randolph's ratification of the Franco-Scottish alliance at the beginning of the Regency was an aggressive act against England. The situation had thus changed from the time when the peace treaty was signed and he was therefore free to support Balliol as the rightful King of Scots. In return for his assistance Balliol agreed that he would be a vassal king, as his father had been, and, within two months of his coronation, he had entirely repudiated the conditions of the peace treaty. Edward was promised large tracts of land along the border which were to be annexed forever to England and which included the town and Castle of Berwick. Balliol also agreed that he would come to England whenever summoned and that failure to comply with the summons would result in a £200,000 fine. Even worse he promised that if this enormous fine were not paid Scotland would revert entirely to the English crown.

While Balliol was actively giving up all that Bruce had won, the Scots chose Sir Andrew Moray as their new Guardian. Sir Andrew was the son of the Moray who had fought and died with Wallace at 'Stirling brig' and had already proved himself a capable soldier. When Balliol moved to Roxburgh Sir Andrew followed but was captured and once again the Scots were leaderless. However in December, the next Guardian, Sir Archibald Douglas, attacked Balliol at Annan and forced him to retreat to Carlisle where he called on Edward for assistance. The English parliament had no wish to embark on another full scale war but Edward acted on his own. Balliol was provided with English troops and set out in March of 1333 to lay siege to Berwick. In May Edward arrived to conduct the campaign in person. Douglas then attempted to distract him by attacking the north of England as Bruce had done. However, unlike his father, Edward refused to abandon his plans for Berwick and Douglas was forced to return or allow the town to fall. On 19 July 1333, he found the English troops drawn up in a strong position on Halidon Hill. There was no alternative to a frontal attack and the resulting battle was almost a Bannockburn in reverse. The Guardian and five Scottish Earls were killed. The Scots were totally defeated, Berwick surrendered and Edward took possession. Balliol marched north meeting little opposition, and again established himself at Perth. The disinherited regained their lands and only a few strongholds held out against them. In June 1334 Balliol made over the promised lands to Edward. The sheriffdoms of Berwick, Roxburgh, Selkirk, Peebles, Edinburgh and Dumfries became part of England.

During the trouble, King David had been sent to Dumbarton for safety and, when Scotland fell to Balliol, the young King sailed for France, where he had been offered sanctuary. John Randolph, the Earl of Moray and Robert Stewart (David's nephew and heir) now took over as joint Guardians and began to recover ground. Most of Southwest Scotland was taken in the summer of 1334 but difficulty was experienced in subduing Galloway. Successful attacks were mounted on the annexed territories on the border and as pressure increased, the English retired to Berwick where they were soon joined by Balliol. Sir Andrew Moray was ransomed around this time. He returned home to take part in the general rising and obtained a spectacular success with the capture of Henry Beaumont and the fall of Buchan.

Most of Scotland had been regained by the autumn when Edward set out from Newcastle in an attempt to restore English supremacy. Roxburgh was rebuilt but little else was achieved and, in the face of French diplomatic pressure, a short truce was concluded in the following year. When it expired in July 1335 two armies set off from England. Edward marched from Carlisle while Balliol led an expedition from Berwick. By August the two forces had reached Perth and had captured John Randolph. Offers of mediation by France and the Pope were rejected and Scottish resistance was largely subdued by the presence of a large English army. Peace talks were held but Sir Andrew Moray refused to submit and was reappointed as Guardian in the spring of 1336. His continued opposition eventually bore fruit and the pressure on Scotland eased when Edward became heavily occupied in France. In the summer of 1338 Edward sailed in pursuit of the French crown and Robert Stewart was appointed to replace Moray who had died of natural causes.

Although the Scottish offensive slackened under the rule of the Steward, the pressure was sustained at a lower level and, with assistance from France, Balliol's supporters were gradually forced out. By the time Edinburgh was retaken in April 1341, it was thought that Scotland was sufficiently safe for King David to return.

David was seventeen years old when he returned to Scotland. For five years there was relatively little discord as he worked to rebuild the administration which had fallen into decay. Then, in the autumn of 1346, the French appealed to Scotland for assistance after Edward's victory at Crecy. David was asked to invade England in an attempt to ease the English pressure on France. He did not hesitate. After mustering an army at Perth the Scots marched south to exact tribute from Westmorland and Cumberland before moving on Durham. There, on a foggy, wet morning in October, they met a highly superior English army and were decisively beaten at Neville's Cross. Many leading Scots were killed and the King himself was captured. He was to remain a prisoner for nearly eleven years.

With Edward now occupied at the siege of Calais, Balliol crossed the border in May of 1347 to recover his losses. There was little resistance, and by the end of the year, his small force had recovered most of Southern Scotland although the castles of Edinburgh, Stirling and Dumbarton prevented him from penetrating into the North. Calais fell soon after but Edward's resources were so depleted that he was unable to force the war with France or with Scotland and a truce was arranged among the three warring nations. The following year saw the first visitation of the Black Death in England. Two years later Scotland became affected. Nearly a third of the population died and the disruption made it impossible to resume any warlike activity. As things returned to normal the draft of a peace treaty was put together but foundered because of Scottish and French action against Berwick. Matters were brought to a head in 1356 when Balliol, who had become increasingly isolated, resigned the Kingdom of Scotland into the hands of the

English crown. Edward set out to once again attempt the reduction of Scotland by force. This time he was fighting, not on behalf of a vassal king, but in an attempt to win the crown for himself. His campaign was similar to his father's last efforts and had as little effect although his journey through Scotland was so devastating that it was remembered as the 'Burnt Candlemas'. He was unable to bring a Scots army to battle and the futility of attempts to take Scotland by force became increasingly obvious. However, with the capture of the King of France at Poitiers, Scotland could no longer look to her continental ally for support and peace became more eagerly desired by both sides. In early October 1357 hostilities were finally concluded by the ratification of a ten year truce. King David was set free in return for a ransom of more than £66,000 which was to be paid in equal instalments throughout the ten years. He returned to Scotland on the 7th October.

Considerable efforts were made to raise the King's ransom. David was granted profits from the sale of wool. Export duties were doubled, trebled and then quadrupled. As a result the burghs increased in importance and it is around this time that 'the three estates', clergy, nobility and burgesses, began to appear in Councils and Parliaments. With the signing of the truce there was a renewal of peaceful trade and communication with England and Scotland began to recover from the administrative disorder which had prevailed during David's imprisonment. It was not long, however, before friction grew up between the King and the Steward who perhaps resented the return of his young uncle. Throughout David's exile, Scotland had been governed by Robert Stewart, as Guardian, with the assistance of the other leading nobles. Within a short time of his return however the King had excluded most of the nobility from his councils. His political advisors consisted mostly of lesser nobles while the burgesses advised him on economic matters. When Queen Joan died in 1362 David proposed to marry the widow of Sir John Logie and this alliance, with the widow of a mere knight, almost led to Civil war. David was "requested" on pain of forcible exile to give up his idea of marriage to Margaret. It is likely that the Lords had genuine cause for complaint but there can be little doubt that Robert Stewart realised that the birth of a son would destroy his favoured position as heir to the kingdom. David refused to give way. He gathered his supporters and made such a show of force that the great "sedition and conspiracy" was immediately crushed. Margaret and David were married on 14 May 1363. The Steward was constrained to submit to the King and promised to be a loyal follower for the rest of his life.

Although great efforts were made to raise the King's ransom, payments stopped after only two instalments were handed over. No reason for the suspension of payment is known but, in the November following David's marriage, negotiations took place regarding the balance. At Westminster two proposals were put forward, both changing the line of succession to the Scottish throne. Edward suggested that Robert Stewart should be bypassed and that David should name either Edward or his son to succeed if he, David, produced no heirs by his new marriage. In return, the balance of the ransom would be cancelled, hostages would be released and occupied territories would be returned. David accepted the treaty and Edward gave up his claim to Scotland recognising David as the rightful King. But when the treaty was discussed at Scone in January of 1364, Parliament would have none of it. Not only would it disinherit a native born Scot who had been recognised as heir to the throne for nearly forty years, but guarantees of Scottish independence would depend largely on English goodwill. Many Scots remembered how Edward's grandfather had acted after the Maid of Norway died and there were no reasons to suspect that the grandson was any more trustworthy.

There was no immediate crisis following the rejection of the English proposal and discussions on the ransom continued. Edward initially requested payment of £100,000 and offered a four year truce but this was considered exorbitant. Alternative proposals were made and the negotiations continued until Edward again became enmeshed in war with France. Finally in 1369, a fourteen year Anglo-Scottish truce was arranged and the ransom was fixed at its initial value, the balance to be paid over the duration of the truce. Just over half the total amount had been paid by the end of the reign.

Throughout the years of his personal rule, David extended the Royal authority on all fronts. He took firm control of financial matters and the measures passed to pay for his ransom helped to increase the Crown's revenue. By the end of his reign all customs were paid to the King and he had persuaded the three estates to allow him to revoke any Royal lands given away since the death of Robert I. Although he took back only a small proportion of these lands the Act of Revocation gave him considerable leverage in dealing with fractious nobles. Their way of life became increasingly subject to Royal domination and not even the Steward was exempt. After a quarrel with Queen Margaret in 1368 he was imprisoned for a short time and a civil war might well have erupted had David not fallen out with his wife and persuaded the bishops to annul their marriage. Her fall from the Royal favour reinstated Robert Stewart who was released and reconciled to the King. David later contemplated a third marriage but died unexpectedly at Edinburgh on 22 February 1371, only eleven days after he had provided his bride to be with a life pension to pay for her trousseau.

Robert II

Born 1316
Reigned: 1371-1390
Son of Walter the 6th High Steward and
Marjorie Bruce, daughter of Robert I
Contemporary of:
Edward III 1327-1377
Richard II 1377-1397
Married:
(1) Elizabeth, daughter of Adam Mure of Rowallan
(2) Euphemia, daughter of Earl of Ross
At least twenty-one children including three surviving sons by
Elizabeth and two sons by Euphemia.
Died at Dundonald, Ayrshire
Buried at Scone

Robert II, the first Stewart King, was descended from Walter Fitzallan, an Anglo Norman, who became High Steward of Scotland under David I in the twelfth century. The family married into the royal line with the union between Robert's father, also Walter, and Marjory Bruce, daughter of Robert I. Declared heir presumptive in 1318 Robert succeeded to the Stewardship when his father died eight years later. He shared the command at Halidon Hill (1333) and was associated in the regency from 1338 to 1341 during King David's exile in France. At Neville's Cross, where the King was captured, Robert retreated — some said deserted — and saved the remnants of the Scots army. He was appointed Guardian of the Kingdom until David's release in 1357. During the next fourteen years there was often friction between the King and his uncle. Robert opposed David on several occasions and was imprisoned for a short time in 1368 but became reconciled and was elevated to the throne when the King died unexpectedly in February 1371.

At fifty-five Robert was already middle aged when he was crowned in March of 1371. He had shown few kingly qualities during his association with the Regency or during

1 Rough Castle, Stirlingshire, a Roman fort on the Antonine wall.

(By permission of the Royal Commission on Ancient Monuments, Scotland.)

2   Cast of a pictish symbol stone from Burghead, Moray.

3   A stone from Drumbuie, Glen Urquhart, showing the common Pictish symbols, the serpent and Z rod, and the spectacles.

4   Pictish symbol stone from Hilton of Cadboll, now in Invergordon
Castle, Ross-shire.

5 Aerial view of the iron-age hillfort of Castlelaw, near Edinburgh.

(Crown copyright: reproduced by permission of the Scottish Development Department.)

6   The soutterain at Castlelaw, near Edinburgh.

(Crown copyright: reproduced by permission of the Scottish Development Department.)

7   The Broch of Mousa, Shetland, typifies an early style of building common in the north and west of Scotland.

(Crown copyright: reproduced by permission of the Scottish Development Department.)

8   Iona Abbey. Burial place of many early kings and centre of the celtic Christian mission.

(Crown copyright: reproduced by permission of the Scottish Development Department.)

9   A group of chessmen found on the Isle of Lewis, an example of Scoto–Viking craft work.

10   A Viking sword hilt found on the island of Eigg.

(Reproduced by permission of the National Museum of Antiquities of Scotland.)

11 An artist's impression of the Monymusk reliquary, in which the relics of St Columba were carried long after his death.
(*Reproduced by permission of the National Museum of Antiquities of Scotland.*)

12 Dunkeld Cathedral, site of the religious and secular headquarters of the kings after 843.

(Crown copyright: reproduced by permission of the Scottish Development Department.)

13   The Round Tower, Abernethy, Perthshire. An early christian
building.

(Crown copyright: reproduced by permission of the Scottish Development Department.)

14   St Rules tower, St. Andrews. An early religious building.

(Crown copyright: reproduced by permission of the Scottish Development Department.)

15   Dunfermline Abbey. Burial place and favourite residence for many of the Canmore line.

(Crown copyright: reproduced by permission of the Scottish Development Department.)

16   Charter of Duncan II to the monks of Durham of lands in south east
Scotland, with his seal attached.

(By permission of the Dean and Chapter of Durham.)

17   St. Andrews Cathedral, begun in the reign of David I, one of the
greatest of the new buildings built to house the new monastic orders
brought to Scotland in the 12th century reorganisation.

18   Caerlaverock Castle — symbolising secular feudalisation with the advent of new landlords.

(Crown copyright: reproduced by permission of the Scottish Development Department.)

19   The Great seal of Alexander III (reverse).
(In the collection of the Duke of Buccleuch and Queensberry, K.T., Bowhill, Selkirk.)

20   The Great seal of Alexander III (obverse).

(In the collection of the Duke of Buccleuch and Queensberry, K.T., Bowhill, Selkirk.)

21   Fifteenth century manuscript of Fordun's Chronica Gentis Scotorum.
Lines 16–24 deal with the death of Alexander II, and thereafter an obituary
of him.

22 The keep of Norham Castle, Northumberland site of the early stages
of the 'Great Cause'.

23   Charter of king John Balliol to his servant William of Silksworth, of
land in Covington, Lanarkshire, with the great seal of King John.

(By permission of the Dean and Chapter of Durham.)

24 Casts of the great seal of Robert I, the Bruce, 1326.
(By kind permission of Archives Nationales, Paris.)

25   Arbroath Abbey, scene of the famous declaration of 1320.

26   A contemporary drawing depicting the coronation of John Balliol from the Chronicle of John of London, circa 1377.

(Reproduced by permission of the British Library.)

27 A contemporary document listing the nineteen conditions of release imposed by Edward III on his captive David II. The drawing celebrates a meeting at Berwick upon Tweed on 3rd October 1357 between representatives of each monarch.

28   Stirling Castle, both castle and town a royal centre for the Jameses.
(Crown copyright: reproduced by permission of the Scottish Development Department.)

29 Threave Castle. The last Douglas stronghold to submit to James II.

(Crown copyright: reproduced by permission of the Scottish Development Department.)

Here begynnys ane litil tretie intitulit the goldyn
targe compilit be Maister Wilyam dunbar

30 Title page of the Golden Targe, Edinburgh: Chepman and Myllar,
1508.

(Reproduced by permission of the Trustees of the National Library of Scotland.)

31   Mary, Queen of Scots, artist unknown.
(Reproduced by permission of the Scottish National Portrait Gallery.)

IACOBVS · I · D · GRATIA ·
REX · SCOTORVM

32 James I, artist unknown.

33   James VI, by Issac Oliver.

(Reproduced by permission of the Scottish National Portrait Gallery.)

the eleven years in which he was Guardian. His lack of ability was to plague him for the rest of his life. Almost as soon as King David died there were rumblings from the Earl of Douglas who claimed kinship with John Balliol. Civil war might have erupted but for the intervention of the Earl of March who persuaded Douglas to give up his rather pretentious claim to the throne. Robert's actions provided a foretaste of his dealings throughout the reign. He rewarded the loyalty of March and placated Douglas with monetary gifts and the hand of his daughter in marriage. Thereafter he would continually seek to reward support instead of taking it as the King's right and would attempt to buy off any opposition.

With his predilection for peace Robert worked to confirm the truce and prevent a return to the wars which had ruined Scotland so often in the past. The defensive alliance with France was renewed and the balance of David's ransom began to be paid. In the first years of his reign the situation remained fairly stable. Concerned about the age of the King and that of his eldest son and heir, John, then nearly 40, the three estates passed a new succession Act assigning the throne to each of Robert's sons and the male descendants of each in order of seniority. England was still involved in the French war and was forced to conclude a truce with Charles V in 1375. However two years later Edward III died and the young, ten year old, Richard was crowned. Charles, taking advantage of the confusion caused by the accession of a minor, broke the truce and invited the Scots to join him in concerted action against England. Although Robert had no wish to see Scotland embroiled in another war his nobles had become increasingly militant. The King's lack of ability to exert strong government and his attempts to buy support had reduced the authority of the crown until it was almost non existent. Many of the nobles had married into the Royal Family and considered that government and law applied only to 'lesser' persons. In many cases their lands on the border were occupied and, with English armies busy on the continent, the nobles were eager for another round of hostilities. Despite the efforts of both governments, a limited war broke out along the border and soon escalated to action at sea. Attempts to quieten affairs resulted in the negotiation of another Anglo-Scottish truce in 1380 and the cancellation of the balance of David's ransom.

The following year saw the domestic unheavals of the Peasants' revolt in England. In Scotland, Prince John, the Earl of Carrick, became associated in the Government with his father but his participation in matters of State did little to quell the martial spirit of the times or to reduce the growing lawlessness which had blossomed under Robert's feeble control. With the Anglo-Scots truce due to expire in 1384 precautions were taken against the renewal of hostilities. Once again Scotland turned to her old ally for assistance and an alliance was concluded whereby French troops and arms would be sent to Scotland if the fighting were resumed. Action was precipitated when an advance party of thirty French knights landed in Scotland in 1384 and joined a border raid on the North of England. They were followed in May 1385 by a much larger force and preparations were made in Edinburgh for a joint expedition to the borders. The company proceeded to Northumberland in the summer but withdrew in the face of an opposing army led by Richard II. To the dismay of the French the Scots refused to fight and followed their now time honoured custom of laying waste to the land ahead of the advancing English army. Although Richard's troops reached and burned Edinburgh, they were unable to fight a decisive action and hunger forced them to retreat. During this campaign monasteries and religious houses were plundered and burnt, largely because of the schism in the Catholic Church. Scotland supported Pope Clement in Avignon while England adhered to Urban who maintained his court at Rome. As a result all religious scruples against attacking clergy were removed and the monasteries suffered. Following Richard's return to England, the French and Scots descended on Cumberland and returned to Scotland with more plunder than ever before. However the war, with its lack of set piece battles in which honour could be won, was not to the liking of the French. Disagreements and bad feelings developed due to the French habit of foraging in the countryside to obtain food, and tempers rose when it became clear that such actions would not be tolerated in Scotland. Eventually, although plans were discussed for an invasion from France, the French Knights decided that there was no place for them in Scotland and sailed home.

The renewal of the border war virtually broke the old King, now almost seventy, and in 1384 the Earl of Carrick, his son and heir, was appointed to rule in his place. Like his father the prince favoured peace but he quickly showed that he was equally unfitted to the task of controlling the unruly nobility and proved himself quite unable to restrict the spreading lawlessness. In 1388 hostilities flared up again with more raids on the north of England. These were generally small scale affairs lasting only a few days but the Scots were spectacularly successful at Otterburn when they captured Henry Hotspur, son and heir of the Earl of Northumberland. Shortly after this action Carrick was removed from the Government and Robert's second son, the Earl of Fife, was installed in his place. Carrick had never been to the liking of the more warlike nobles and his growing infirmity, caused by a kick from a horse, provided the excuse to replace him. The Earl of Fife had planned and led the last expeditions in person. He was much more belligerent than either his father or his elder brother, had already proved himself in warfare and had shown sound judgment and strength of purpose in administering his own lands. He was to be effective ruler of Scotland for nearly thirty years. Appointed as Guardian of the realm in December of 1388 he had hardly began to settle into the task when King Robert died in the following April at his Castle in Ayrshire. His peaceful and dignified nature had been quite misplaced in such a turbulent age. Although Robert invariably held Scotland's interest at heart he had been singularly unsuccessful in exerting the Royal authority and had little influence over the events of his reign. His successor would prove to be no better.

Robert III

Born c 1337
Reigned: 1390-1406
Eldest son of Robert II
Contemporary of:
Richard II 1377-1399
Henry IV 1399-1413
Married Annabella Drummond, daughter of Sir John Drummond
of Stobhall
Three sons, four daughters and two illegitimate sons
Died at Rothesay, Isle of Bute
Buried in Paisley Abbey

On the death of his father in April 1390, Prince John, the Earl of Carrick, ascended the throne and immediately changed his name to Robert. John was considered a most unlucky name for a king, having been borne by John Balliol and John II of France, both of whom lost their thrones. Robert's efforts to evade the fates were to no avail. Before the end of his reign he was to exclaim to his Queen that she might write on his tomb the words, "Here lies the worst of Kings and the most wretched of men in the whole realm".

Robert was nearly fifty-three years old when he succeeded to the throne and was already a semi-invalid, having been kicked by a horse, possibly in 1388. In temperament he was gentle, dignified and courteous, in fact rather like his father. Although associated with Robert II in the administration of Scotland between 1381 and 1384, he had taken no physical part in the war with England and had been effectively removed from the government only months before his father died. His succession was perceived as a continuation of the lax rule which had allowed the spread of lawlessness. Civil disorder increased even before he was crowned. "Wyld wykkyd Heland-men", descended on the more 'civilised' lowland areas and the northern lords were not slow to use them in settling their disputes. In a feud with the Bishop of Moray, the Wolf of Badenoch burned the towns of Forres and Elgin and tore down the cathedral. As he was the King's brother little action was taken against him and the rapacity of the highland clans increased. For two years in succession, Angus suffered from their marauding tactics and not even knights in armour could keep them under control. The year of 1396 even saw the spectacle of a formal clan duel at Perth. Thirty men of the Clan Chattan faced an equal number from the Clan Kay and fought until only a dozen were left alive. By 1397 the general council at Stirling were declaiming against the "great and horrible destruccions" which had occurred and it was said that "there was no law in Scotland but he who was stronger oppressed him who was weaker and the whole realm was a den of thieves and murderers".

Although matters at home had deteriorated steadily, foreign relations were better than they had been for a century. The borders were policed in an attempt to stop the intermittent raiding which had occurred during the previous reign and safe conducts were freely issued to travellers between the two countries. Trading improved and social relationships were restored as knights travelled to and fro to visit the tournaments which had become highly popular.

By 1397 the King's eldest son, David, Earl of Carrick, was nineteen years old. When he began to gain authority as the heir apparent, he fell out with his uncle, the Earl of Fife, who had exercised considerable power during the previous reign and continued to do so under Robert III. In an attempt to placate them, both were raised to the rank of Duke, a title which was well established in France but had never been seen before in Scotland. The heir apparent was made Duke of Rothesay and his uncle was created Duke of Albany, the title by which he is best known. However the new social status they enjoyed did nothing to reduce the friction and, with a quite ineffectual king, two parties developed, one led by Rothesay and the Queen, the other by Albany. Matters came to a head in 1399 at a general council held in Perth. In an attempt to limit Albany's power, Rothesay appears to have been instrumental in persuading the council to declare that, "the misgovernance of the realm and the default of the keeping of the common law should be attributed to the King and his officers". It seems that the declaration was aimed primarily at Albany, the chief officer, rather than at the King. Robert was given the opportunity to summon his officers and, "accuse them in presence of his council", but instead he preferred to take the blame on his own shoulders. The end result was his virtual deposition. Rothesay, being heir apparent, was appointed to be the King's lieutenant, but a check was placed on his powers by the creation of a special council of twenty-one "wyse men" with whom he was to consult. Albany, as the chief councillor, remained very much to the fore. Thereafter the King took very little part in the government and retired to virtual seclusion on his private estates.

For the next three years, until 1402, Scotland was under the nominal control of the Duke of Rothesay. In England, Richard II was deposed by his cousin Henry Bolingbroke and, within a year, was 'found' dead in Berkeley Castle. Although Scotland was deeply shocked by the usurpation, relations between the two countries had been steadily improving and the peace treaty was ratified with the new English monarch. However, in both countries there were parties which favoured war and hostilities were initiated when Rothesay angered the Scottish Earl of March by refusing to honour his betrothal to March's daughter. The Earl appealed to Henry IV, his fourth cousin, for assistance in avenging this slight on the family name. Although Henry was unwilling to take direct action, the Percy family in Northumberland was less reluctant. Joining up with a force brought south by March, Henry Hotspur led the Percies over the border only to be pushed back by the Earl of Douglas. The reverse so infuriated the English that Henry was forced into action. He advanced to Newcastle and, in August 1400, sent a letter to Robert, still nominally the King of Scotland. Robert was reminded that the Kings of England were, and always had been, the superior lords of Scotland. He was, "required, counselled and exhorted", to do homage for the Kingdom with the threat that, if his homage were not forthcoming, "we should be provoked to stretch forth the

Arm of our Might". Robert probably never saw the letter which was dealt with by Rothesay. There was never any possibility of a Scots submission and Henry was 'provoked' to march on Edinburgh. Although the town was burned it proved impossible to subdue the castle. Indeed the campaign appears to have been undertaken with a view to demonstrating Henry's might rather than in an attempt to subdue the Kingdom. The palace of Holyrood was spared and, throughout the long march, the English acted with moderation, granting safe conducts freely and sparing life whenever possible. But the weather in late August was terrible and the English army was plagued by lack of food. With the Welsh rising against him under Owen Glendower, Henry retired south in September and a short truce was arranged at the end of the year. Peace negotiations in the following year broke down when Henry suggested that the Pope should adjudicate on the question of homage and received a rejoinder asking if his own claim to the English throne might be subjected to similar arbitration!

Rothesay fell from power in 1402, having overstretched the authority assigned to him when his father relinquished control of the government. Three of his chief supporters, the Queen, the third Earl of Douglas and Bishop Trail of St. Andrews, died between Christmas 1400 and Autumn 1401. His special council, turned against him and resigned because he consistently ignored their advice. Increasingly isolated, he made the final mistake of attempting to take over the castle which had fallen vacant when Bishop Trail died. This was evidently the last straw. He was arrested and confined to Falkland Castle where he died in March 1402. Dysentry was named as the official cause of his death but rumours of foul play were rife and, in a general Council held in May, Albany was accused of plotting to regain power. He insisted that Rothesay had been arrested for the public good and that he had died of natural causes. The council sessions were long and stormy but, in the end, Albany was exonerated and a declaration was issued that Rothesay, "departed from this life through the divine providence and not otherwise".

With Rothesay's death, Albany was restored to power, now acting essentially as Regent for the young Prince James who became heir apparent at the age of eight. Almost immediately trouble flared up on the borders and the international situation became confused as England drifted into Civil War. Henry IV was fighting to preserve his crown against the families of Percy and Mortimer and was hampered by the Welsh rising which was not finally crushed until 1410. In Scotland a person claiming to be Richard II appeared stating that he had escaped from his English prison. Albany received him graciously and, although remaining non-committal,he did little to dissuade the Scots nobles from fighting against Henry on the Percy-Mortimer side. Indeed Scots were present on both sides. Border feuding increased and Albany's son was captured at the battle of Homildon Hill along with "the flower of chivalry" of Scotland. His imprisonment ensured that the bogus Richard could not be used as a figurehead for promoting English revolution. In 1403 Henry Hotspur was killed at Shrewsbury and the Percy rebellion was effectively crushed. However, Henry's success in bringing the Civil War to a temporary conclusion did nothing to quell the martial spirit of the Scots Lords. As both sides became increasingly belligerent Robert III began to have fears for the safety of his son, Prince James. In addition to the possibility of an outbreak of full scale war Robert must have realised that only he and the Prince stood between Albany and the throne. He decided that James should be sent to the safety of France and, in the spring of 1406, the Prince sailed from North Berwick with the Earl of Orkney. His ship was captured by English privateers off Flamborough Head and, although Orkney and most of his followers were set free, James was sent to the Tower. The news of his capture broke the old King's heart. He was then nearly seventy, and, in his grief, he refused to eat. On Palm Sunday, 1406, he died in his castle at Rothesay on the Isle of Bute.

THE GLORY OF THE STEWARTS

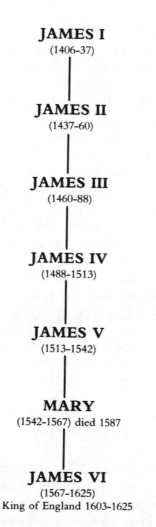

JAMES I
(1406–37)

JAMES II
(1437–60)

JAMES III
(1460–88)

JAMES IV
(1488–1513)

JAMES V
(1513–1542)

MARY
(1542–1567) died 1587

JAMES VI
(1567–1625)
King of England 1603–1625

THE LATER STEWARTS

The long and troublesome minorities of the later Stewarts provide the most apparent thread to link the events of the two hundred years between the reigns of James I and James VI. Of the seven monarchs who reigned during that period, all but one succeeded to the throne as immature children. James I was approaching his twelfth birthday when his father died. Detained as a captive in England he did not return to Scotland until almost eighteen years had passed. His son, James II, succeeded him at the age of six. James III was only eight years old when his father was murdered and, although James IV had reached his majority by the time he came to the throne, he was still at the relatively tender age of fifteen years. Killed in battle when he had reached the peak of his powers, the Kingdom was inherited by James V, then only 17 months old. Mary, Queen of Scots, was born six days before her father died and she, in turn, was forced to abdicate in favour of her son James VI who was crowned when he was just over a year old.

The strength of the monarchy in the 15th and 16th centuries depended largely on the power and prestige of the reigning monarch. When the King was weak, or under age, good government declined, the powerful nobles jockeyed for position, and law and order all but vanished. Private feuds sprang up so that, when the King reached his majority, he usually found the royal finances depleted and the country in the hands of men who were reluctant to relinquish the reins of power. The problems must not, however, be exaggerated. James VI certainly inherited a more secure crown than James I and, despite the struggle with the nobility, and in particular with the House of Douglas, which marked the 15th century, disorder and anarchy were gradually put down.

Scotland was not alone in suffering internal problems caused by an over powerful nobility. England faced the same difficulties, although perhaps not to the same degree, and the long minority of Henry VI and the Wars of the Roses served to curb Plantagenet ambitions to annexe their northern neighbour. For many years there was peace, of sorts, between the two countries but, despite one or two faltering steps in the opposite direction, Scotland and France remained united in common fear and distrust of England. Scotland gained culturally from the Auld Alliance which planted some, "lilies in the cauld kail-yard", but it became increasingly obvious that the material and military benefits were reaped almost entirely by France. Disenchantment set in and, as "the richt way to the Kingdome of Hevine", became the burning question of the day, Scotland turned towards the reformed faith. The links with France were further weakened by religious differences and by the overwhelming and distrusted influence which the French exercised in Scotland during the regency of Marie of Guise. By the time Mary, Queen of Scots, returned to Scotland her country had become officially Protestant and looked more and more to the Protestant Queen of England for support.

James VI, baptised as a Catholic, was brought up in the Protestant faith and in the hope, and expectation, of succeeding to the English throne. In 1603 Elizabeth died and James was invited south. The transition was complete.

James I
Born July 1394
Reigned: 1406-1437
Second son of Robert III
Married Joan Beaufort, daughter of Duke of Somerset and first
cousin to Henry V
Two sons (twins) and six daughters
Contemporary of:
Henry IV 1399-1413
Henry V 1413-1422
Henry VI 1422-1461 and 1470-1471
Died (murdered) in the Dominican Priory, Perth.
Buried in the Church of the Charterhouse, Perth.

Although not the first Stewart King, James I can certainly be ranked as the first of the great Stewarts. He became heir apparent in 1402 when his elder brother died. Four years later attempts were made to send him to France because of the steadily deteriorating situation in Scotland. Captured, en route, by English privateers he was taken to the Tower of London and spent the next eighteen years in captivity before returning to Scotland in 1424.

His father, Robert III, died shortly after receiving news of his capture and, when Parliament met in June of 1406, the young prince was immediately recognised as King James I. Albany, now heir presumptive, was appointed to be the Governor of the Realm. For over fourteen years Albany had been associated with the administration of Scotland but, as Governor, he obtained greater power than he had ever wielded on previous occasions. "He seymt to be a mychty king" and had a great seal struck for his personal use showing him with all the trappings of Royalty. Documents issued under the seal were dated, not by the year of James' accession, but according to the year of Albany's Governorship and he was wont to refer to himself as Governor, "by the grace of God" and to write of "his" subjects. As heir presumptive he entertained hopes of eventually succeeding to the throne itself and, although there was never any direct effort to supplant the King, Albany showed no eagerness to obtain James' release from captivity.

The Governor's relationship with Henry IV drifted between cordiality and veiled hostility. In various letters Henry referred to him as "our dearest Kinsman", but in others, when the relationship was less friendly, Albany was, "Governor, as he asserts, of the realm of Scotland". Initially, at least, the Governor's actions were largely influenced by the fact that his son, Murdoch, had been captured at Homildon Hill and was held captive in England. The Anglo-Scottish truce was renewed from year to year and the two countries avoided significant belligerent actions until just before Albany's death in 1420.

Internally, however, matters were very different. The growing power of the nobles during the previous two reigns had significant effects in reducing the authority of the central government and this was nowhere more apparent than in the Isles. These had been brought under Scottish control by Alexander III and, although the Islesmen had supported Bruce in the struggle for independence, their loyalty had been given to Bruce personally rather than to the institution of the monarchy. With the lack of strong leadership after Bruce died, the Isles had reverted almost to the position of a semi independent state. Indeed, in various treaties signed between England and France and their respective allies, Donald, Lord of the Isles, had added his signature independently of the Scots King and appears to have signed as an ally of England. Donald, from whom the clan MacDonald takes its name, was descended from Somerled who had first wrested the Western Isles from the Norwegians. In addition to his control of the Islands he wielded considerable authority on the North West mainland and, through marriage, obtained a claim on the earldom of Ross. When the Earl of Ross died in 1402 the lands passed to his young daughter Euphemia, Donald's niece and Albany's grand-daughter. Donald's wife was next in line to the earldom and it might have seemed reasonable that he should be appointed as the young girl's guardian. However Albany had other ideas and, by 1405, was styling himself "Lord of the Ward of Ross". A few years later Euphemia was 'persuaded' to resign her rights to the earldom and it seemed likely that it would be given, not to Donald, but to Albany's son the Earl of Buchan. Donald was apparently accepted as the rightful heir within Ross itself and, in the face of what was perceived by the MacDonalds as Albany's perfidy, he attempted to make good his claim by the use of force. Swearing to "subdew the Brugh of Aberdene, Mearns, Angus and all Fife to the Forth", Donald seized Inverness and marched through Moray towards the East Coast. By mid July, 1411, he had arrived at Harlaw, only twenty miles from Aberdeen. There he was checked by the Earl of Mar who had raised the local levies to defend the City and the relatively civilised areas to the south. The conflict of Red Harlaw was fought with what, for the time, were full scale armies. It is commonly described as a struggle between highland savagery and lowland civilisation and, of all the civil conflicts between Scot and Scot, Red Harlaw was certainly the fiercest. After the battle both sides claimed victory. However, although the outcome of the day's fighting was, to some extent, inconclusive Donald was unable to make good his threat to subdue the East coast region and retired to the Isles. The lowlands were saved and Albany acted with vigour to remove any further threats. He quickly recovered Dingwall Castle in the Province of Ross and, in the following year, raised three armies to subdue the Isles. There is no record of their movements during 1412 but, before the end of the year, Donald submitted, gave up his claim to Ross, and handed over hostages to ensure that he would keep the peace. Although the battle of Harlaw clearly prevented the spread of Celtic influence outside the north west it had relatively little effect on the status of the Isles or on the earldom of Ross. Donald still claimed to be "Lord of the foresaid Isles and of the earldom of Ross" and, in a truce arranged between England and France in 1416, Donald appears as an ally of both countries!

The year 1413 saw the creation of Scotland's first

University at St. Andrews. The need for a University had been recognised as early as 1400 and a foundation charter had been issued in 1411 by the Bishop of St. Andrew's. Authority to confer Master's degrees was obtained two years later when the Bull of Pope Benedict XIII arrived in Scotland. There could be little doubt that the new University was amply justified by the academic needs of Scottish scholars. The wars and plagues of the fourteenth century had forced those seeking an education to look for it abroad. Scots had studied at most of the major continental universities and were present in sufficiently large numbers at some of these to have their own student associations. However the University of St. Andrews was also intended to check the spread of heresy. By the beginning of the century the Lollards, who based their ideas on the teachings of John Wycliffe, had begun to spread North into Scotland. Although the movement never became highly popular, Bishop Wardlaw, of St. Andrews, was sufficiently concerned to indicate in 1411 that one of the advantages of the University would be to provide "an impregnable wall of doctors and masters — to withstand heresies and errors". Four years after the University was founded the students who were about to graduate were required to swear an oath to "defend the King against the attack of Lollards".

In the year that St. Andrews was set up Henry IV died. His son Henry V succeeded at a time when France had become embroiled in a Civil War and, anxious to obtain as much advantage as possible from the internal struggle in France, he attempted to secure the neutrality of the Scots so that they would not interfere with his continental ambitions. Negotiations were set in motion to discuss the possibility of a new truce and the release of Albany's son Murdoch. Near his death Henry IV had suggested it was time that King James should be released but his son no doubt considered the captive king of Scots to be of too much political advantage to be released just as England was about to go to war. The negotiations dragged on until, in 1415, Henry sailed to France having already stated his claim to the French crown.

His outstanding success at Agincourt so worried the Scottish Government that, when he returned to England for reinforcements, the Scots published the treaty of Northampton in which Henry's great grandfather, Edward II, had given up all claims to the overlordship of Scotland. The apparent invincibility of English arms and the ever present worry that he might turn his attention to Scotland caused relationships to become tense. The concern was only slightly relieved by the release of Murdoch in 1416. When Henry returned to France the next year the Scots undertook to besiege Roxburgh and Berwick but achieved no success and later styled their humiliation at Berwick as the "Foul Raid". The following year brought an appeal from the Dauphin for assistance and, in 1419, Albany's son, the Earl of Buchan, was sent to France with seven thousand Scottish men at arms. When the Scots expeditionary force proved too small to be effective Buchan returned to raise another force of 5000 men which embarked for France in 1421. To counter the entry of Scottish troops on the French side Henry brought James to France in a vain attempt to show the troops that their King was fighting alongside the English. James could not, of course, refuse to accompany him but made it clear that he had no intention of trying to stop his subjects fighting for the Dauphin. In 1421 Buchan routed and killed Henry's brother, the Duke of Clarence, in Anjou. It was the first serious reverse which the invading army had experienced. The victory did much to raise French morale and incensed Henry who thereafter refused quarter to any captured Scots. Soon after this defeat Henry died of St. Fiacre's disease. St. Fiacre (or Fergus) was said to have been the son of a Scottish King and, on learning the name of his illness, Henry is reported to have railed against the Scots with the outburst, "wherever I go, I find these Scots in my beard, alive or dead". England passed to the King's baby son, Henry VI, and for the next four years the war continued with varying success until Joan of Arc appeared and brought the French to final victory.

Albany died in 1420 leaving his son Murdoch in control.

He showed little aptitude for government and the Scots began to wish for the return of the King. At the same time the death of Henry V made it politically expedient for the English to release James who had grown up in England and had become personally friendly with the leading English nobility. James had also fallen in love with Joan Beaufort, the grand-daughter of John of Gaunt, and it was hoped that his return to Scotland might leave England free to deal with France without the possibility of Scottish interference. Negotiations were conducted for his release in 1423. No ransom was to be levied, because James was not a prisoner of war, but £40,000 was claimed as expenses for the costs incurred during his residence in England. In February the following year James and Joan were married at Southwark. A seven year truce was concluded at the end of March and "betwene Mersh and Averill" the newly married couple rode North over the border. After nearly eighteen years of captivity James entered Scotland to claim his inheritance.

Of middle height, powerfully built and with a shock of reddish hair, James quickly showed his subjects that the long years of captivity had not been wasted. In England he had been given an education befitting his rank and was well schooled in the cultural pursuits of his day. He spoke English and French and was probably familiar with Latin. His love of music and the arts became well known and he is justly renowned for the quality of his major poem, The Kingis Quair (the King's book), a love poem which clearly shows the influence of Chaucer. His physical education had not been neglected. He was a skilled horseman and was said to have excelled in all athletic pursuits. In particular he was an expert at putting the weight and throwing the hammer.

Even more important than this knightly education was the knowledge he grasped of government from his association with the leaders of England. He soon realised that the lawlessness in Scotland had developed because of the lack of a strong central authority and determined to remedy affairs by decisive action. "If God grant me life", he said, "there shall be no place in my realm where the key shall not keep the castle and the bracken bush the cow". Throughout his reign James acted continually to break the power of the nobles and to enhance the Royal authority. The church was reformed, agriculture was improved and trade was encouraged. James got through an impressive amount of legislation and made sure that it would bear fruit by avoiding international entanglements. The peace with England was preserved and Scotland was strengthened by foreign alliances.

No attempt was made to secure the friendship of the nobility and the antagonisms caused by the King's burning desire to limit their power would eventually cause his downfall. Even before his coronation in May 1424 he arrested the eldest surviving son of Duke Murdoch. The specific reasons for the arrest are not clear but it provided a clear warning that Murdoch's family were no longer above the law. Parliament, meeting soon after the coronation, passed acts which clearly showed the mood of the King. Private wars were forbidden and a limit was set on the size of retinue accompanying travelling nobles. To increase the Royal finances and ensure that the crown had the money to put his ideas into force James made an effort to restore the depleted treasury. An inquiry was launched into the status of lands which had belonged to the crown during the reign of David II but which had since been granted to others. The obvious intention was to repossess these estates and the current owners were required to produce charters giving proof of their rightful ownership. Rebel lands were, in the future, to be forfeited to the crown whereas previously they had descended, in the normal manner, to the heirs of the outlawed rebel. The payment of grants or pensions from customs duties was forbidden and this money was granted to the King, ostensibly to pay for the expenses incurred during his captivity in England. For similar reasons a tax of one shilling in the pound was levied on land rents. This forerunner of the modern income tax was, however, soon dropped because of widespread resentment. Other acts of the first parliament dealt with the public weal and with defense. Wolves were to be hunted down and rookeries destroyed.

Begging was forbidden except for those who had no other way of earning a living. Men with no land to support themselves were encouraged to seek work under threat of banishment or "burning on the cheek". Weapons, suitable to their rank in society, were to be obtained by every man and inspections were to be held four times a year. Archery was encouraged. All men were to practice with the bow. Football and golf were prohibited!

Within a year of this parliament the King again moved against the Albanys. Possibly to forestall a coup d'etat, or because of a long standing resentment against the Albany family for their involvement in the death of the Duke of Rothesay and their reluctance to obtain his own release from England, James arrested Duke Murdoch and others of his family on a charge of high treason. Before Murdoch could be brought to trial, one son who remained at liberty burned Dumbarton in defiance and this probably sealed their fate. In May 1425 Duke Murdoch, two of his sons, and his father-in-law, the Earl of Lennox, were beheaded. At a stroke James had completely crushed the most powerful noble family, indeed the family which had run the government of Scotland during all the years of his captivity.

Two years later he decided to apply the same remedy to the Isles. The example he had meted out to Albany had little effect in the Isles where "Hieland men commonly reft and slew ilk an utheris" (robbed and slew one another). Parliament normally met at Perth, which had virtually become the capital, but in 1427 James summoned the estates to meet him in Inverness and called on the Highland Chiefs to attend him there. When they arrived he immediately arrested forty of them and threw them into prison. Three were quickly tried and executed but most of the others were released. Alexander, Lord of the Isles, was among those who were permitted to return to their homelands but the, "lovely advice", he was given before his departure had no effect. In the following year he raised an army numbering about 10,000 and destroyed Inverness, the scene of his humiliation. James retaliated and utterly defeated him in Lochaber in June

1429. At the end of August Alexander appeared penitent before the King in Holyrood Abbey. With the intervention of Queen Joan, his life was spared and he suffered only a short time in prison. Two years later Alexander's cousin, Donald Balloch, again raided the Isles, and defeated a Royal Army led by the Earl of Mar, victor of Harlaw. As James himself prepared to take the field Donald had second thoughts and fled to Ireland. His departure signalled the end of resistance and there was little further trouble.

With the Albanys gone and the Isles tranquil, the King continued to work through Parliament to strengthen his country and to give his subjects a just peace. At the same time he lost no opportunity to increase the Royal revenues. The border estates of the Earl of March were forfeited to the crown because his father had sided with the English during the previous reign. When the Earl of Mar died in 1435 his earldom, and the lands associated with it reverted to the crown. Indeed, by 1436, the twin processes of forfeiture and reversion had brought the Crown the earldoms of March, Fife, Lennox, Mar, Buchan and Ross. The independent great earldoms were held by the King's relations or (apparently) close friends and it seemed that James had achieved his desire to make the crown the pre-eminent power in the country. Twin boys, born in 1430 secured the succession. The truce with England had been preserved and the alliance with France had been strengthened by the marriage of the King's daughter to the Dauphin. In the early years of his reign James had leant more towards England than France but with these two countries embroiled in a fierce war, there was concern over the English intentions towards Scotland. James' efforts in 1427 to transfer the truce with England into a lasting peace had been unsuccessful and the alternative proposal which the French made regarding the linking of the Royal families by marriage seemed to provide a bulwark against the possibility of the renewal of the old English claim to overlordship of Scotland. Attempts by the English fleet to capture the ship carrying Princess Margaret to France increased the concern and led to retaliation by the Scots.

Berwick was unsuccessfully besieged and an English force from the northern provinces took the opportunity to cross the border. After it was defeated in Berwickshire James turned his attention to Roxburgh, which was then in England hands. He started a siege but suddenly, and for no obvious reason, broke away and returned north.

The inglorious and humiliating attempts to take Berwick and Roxburgh in 1436 marked the turning point in James' career. Previously, as he acquired power at the expense of the nobility through diplomatic means and the due process of law, he had been unassailable but his first entry to the area of warfare had shown him to be vulnerable. He was no longer the athletic young man who had ridden back to Scotland with his newlywed bride in 1424. His desire to bring order and peace to Scotland had perhaps endeared him to the common people but the ruthlessness with which he had curbed the power of the nobility had done much to alienate him from this sector of society. A further source of resentment lay in his lack of attention to the expenses which were still owed to England. When he returned from captivity many hostages were sent to England to ensure payment. However, although the Royal coffers had been swelled through taxes, customs and the acquisition of land, James had made little attempt to pay off the outstanding amounts and many hostages, all of noble birth, were still exiled. Some had even died in England. The effects of these resentments were apparent at Roxburgh where there was "detestable schism and most wicked division sprung from envy" and it is probable that the gathering of the nobles in the full panoply of war made them sense that they still had the power to regain their former glory.

The conspiracy which led to James' murder in the following year had its roots in events spread over many years. Sir Robert Graham, the leader of the plot, had nursed a secret enmity for more than ten years. Graham had been arrested after Albany's son was imprisoned in 1424 but had later been released. He had never forgiven James for his imprisonment and his anger against the King had been fanned when the earldom of Strathearn had been taken from his nephew who was sent to England in 1427 as a hostage. Associated with him in the murder plot was Walter Stewart, the King's Uncle and Earl of Athol, and Athol's grandson, Sir Robert Stewart the Chamberlain. These two had various grievances. Walter's son had been given as a hostage when James returned to Scotland and had died in exile. However, the destruction of the Albanys had brought the Athol family very close to the crown and until James' sons were born the older Athol had been recognised as heir presumptive. One of the twins died in infancy and there was now only one young boy between Athol and the throne. James never suspected them of disaffection and they gave no hint of it. Indeed it is possible that they remained loyal to the King until approached by Graham and until a "spaewife", possibly paid by Graham, prophesied that they would wear the crown within a year.

The King spent Christmas at the Dominican priory situated just outside the walls of Perth. He stayed on until February, and on the night of the 20th, spent a quiet evening playing chess before his courtiers left him to prepare for bed. As he was standing before the fire there was the sound of a scuffle outside his door and a cry of treason. Sir Robert Stewart had admitted Graham and other conspirators. While Lady Catherine Douglas barred the door by thrusting her arm into the slots which should have held the missing bar, James hid in a large sewer running under the room. The sewer opened to the outside but its entrance had been sealed only a few days before on the orders of the King who had lost several tennis balls in its depths. Before the traitors broke into his room the Queen and her ladies had time to cover the hole James had ripped open in the floor. Not finding him the conspirators departed but returned when one of them remembered the sewer. Entering it they discovered the King who was unarmed. He fought bitterly for his life in the enclosed space but there could be no doubt of the outcome. When removed from his hiding place he was found to be dead "with twenty-eight wounds, most toward the heart".

The conspirators were all captured within a month. There was no popular rising on the death of the King as Graham seems to have expected and the only gain of the traitors was torture and death. James was buried in the Church of the Charterhouse in Perth. His heart was taken on pilgrimage to the Holy Land but was returned to Scotland in 1443 by one of the Knights of St. John.

James II
Born October 1430
Reigned: 1437-1460
Younger (twin) son of James I
Married Mary, daughter of Duke of Gueldres and niece of Duke of Burgundy
Four sons and two daughters
Contemporary of Henry VI, 1422-1461 and 1470-1471
Died (by exploding cannon) at Roxburgh
Buried in Holyrood Abbey, Edinburgh

"James of the fiery face", so called because of a conspicuous birthmark, was the younger of twin sons born to Queen Joan and James I on 16th October, 1430. The elder of the twins, Alexander, died in infancy and James had no other male children. When his father was murdered the young King was only seven years old and the years of his minority saw the breakdown of the Royal authority which had been established during the previous reign. Later, as he matured, he followed his father's example in dealing with the nobility and much of his personal rule was concerned with overcoming the powerful Douglas family.

Previous coronations had taken place at Scone, near the town of Perth from which James I had conducted most of the government. Scone, however, was considered to be too close to the disorderly Highlands where Sir Robert Graham had achieved a strong following and tradition was broken with the young King's coronation at Edinburgh, on 25 March 1437.

After the coronation Queen Joan was given the custody of the Royal children and took them to live with her in Edinburgh Castle. The government however was shared between Archibald, the fifth Earl of Douglas, who was made Lieutenant General, or Guardian, and Bishop Cameron, James I's chancellor. Douglas had a good record of support and friendship for James I. He was a nephew of the old king and claimed to be heir presumptive. Initially Parliament attempted to follow the policies set out in the previous reign. A new truce was concluded with England, to run until 1447, and the dangers of a Royal minority were recognised when it was ordained that no "landis nor possessionis pertenyng to the King be gewyn nor grantit till any man without the avisioun and consent of the thre Estatis". However no amount of well meant legislation could stop the scramble for power and it was later said that "so lang as the King is young, great men reignis at their awin libertie".

The first bid for power was made by Sir William Crichton, the governor of Edinburgh Castle and a trusted servant of the dead King. He seized the Royal revenues and forbade Queen Joan access to her son. Crichton may have been acting purely from ambition but it is possible that he felt Joan's English connections, she was the cousin of Henry V, would prove to be a bad influence on the young King. Joan, who no doubt expected to have some say in the Government, retaliated by spiriting the boy out of the castle concealed in her luggage. She left with the stated intention of making a pilgrimage to the White Kirk of Our Lady of Lothian but, instead, took her son to Stirling Castle to Sir Andrew Livingstone, another trusted servant of James I. Sir Andrew proposed to march on Edinburgh against Crichton and both appealed to Douglas, the Guardian, for aid. However Douglas appeared quite indifferent to their quarrel and rather than resort to armed conflict, they patched up their differences to work together in an uneasy alliance. Crichton replaced Bishop Cameron as Chancellor and Livingstone was named Guardian of the King. In the summer of 1439 Douglas died of the plague which had returned to Scotland. Queen Joan, finding herself in the middle of a struggle for power, and without the protection of Douglas, remarried, but was immediately arrested by Livingstone to prevent the power inherent in the Queen's name from being transferred to an outsider. In order to secure her release Joan was constrained to give Livingstone custody of her son and to formally absolve him of the insult of her arrest. The King now remained with Livingstone but, in the following year, during a hunting trip, he was ambushed, or 'rescued', by Crichton who took him from Stirling to Edinburgh. Civil war was only averted by the intervention of the Bishops of St. Andrews and Moray who persuaded the two protagonists to come to terms. The example set by Crichton and Livingstone served to encourage the breakdown of law and order. The right to private war was renewed and, with an outbreak of famine and the plague, it seemed as if there was "nothing but conspiracies, treason (and) troubles".

The death of the fifth Earl of Douglas did not however leave Scotland open to complete control by Crichton and Livingstone. Archibald was succeeded in the Earldom by his son William who, although only sixteen, was much more spirited and aggressive than his father. As the greatest land-owner in the country he saw his estates as a semi-independent Kingdom within the realm and proclaimed himself "sovereign within his marches", declaring that his vassals need not obey the King's commands. He was now the first male in the line of succession to the throne and obviously aspired to the position of Lieutenant General which had not been filled since his father's death during the previous year. Crichton and Livingstone removed this threat to their assumption of total power by a bold and simple act of treachery. William and his brother were invited to Edin-burgh so that the Chancellor would have the 'benefit' of their counsel. Despite warnings the two brothers accepted the invitation and rode to Edinburgh Castle where they dined on 24 November, 1440. After a pleasant meal both were seized and summarily beheaded on Castle Hill. The young King James was shocked at this treatment of his guests but his objections had no effect and he was thrust aside.

The "black dinner" certainly broke the power of the Douglas family but its effects were purely temporary and the revival of their strength was to exact a bitter vengeance which came near to toppling James' crown. When William and his brother were executed their lands passed to their grand-uncle, James Douglas (the Gross). With his "four stone of talch (fat) and mair", James was in no mood to fight a blood feud over the executions which had brought him his inheritance. Until his death in 1443 he enjoyed his estates quietly and the threat from the Douglas family was not renewed until he was succeeded by his son, the eighth Earl.

During the remaining years of the King's minority, foreign affairs proceeded very satisfactorily but the ever present friction between Crichton and Livingstone resulted in a continuation of the spread of lawlessness and anarchy at home. The Auld Alliance was strengthened by the marriage of the King's sister, Isobel, to the Duke of Brittany. Problems with the Hanseatic towns, which had been troubled by Scottish pirates, were straightened out and negotiations were undertaken with Bremen, Hamburg and other towns to improve foreign trade. Other continental alliances were sought and obtained and relationships with the Netherlands, a continuing outlet for Scottish goods, were improved by the marriage of one of James' sisters to the Lord of Campvere.

In Scotland itself the government proved largely ineffective because of the continuing power struggles among the leading noble families. There was also confusion within the church caused, once again, by two Popes setting themselves up in opposition to each other. During the previous schism Scotland had allied itself to one Pope but on this occasion there were conflicting attitudes, and the arguments within the Church brought it into disrepute. It must have seemed that the last vestiges of stability were about to fall and the problems within the Church were reflected in the anarchy in society. The Estates attempted to resolve matters in 1443 when they met at Stirling. It was ordained that "ferme and fast obedieince be kepit till our haly fadir the Pope Eugenne" and that such obedience should not be altered unless "the King and the realm ordane and decrete therapone". This intervention by the state into church affairs helped to restore order among the clergy but the healing of the wounds caused by the schism was accompanied by a new power struggle in secular affairs. When James the Gross died he was succeeded by his son William who was determined to regain the Lieutenant Generalship which had not been filled since the fifth Earl died. Livingstone and Crichton had maintained a facade of mutual aid despite many squabbles but soon after James the Gross died Livingstone broke away and proclaimed himself innocent of the events which had culminated in the "black dinner". He and Douglas then formed an alliance and proceeded to oust Crichton who was denounced as a rebel at a General Council held in October 1444. By that time Douglas seems to have achieved his ambition of becoming recognised as the Lieutenant General and in the years of 1444 and 1445 there was considerable feuding between the Crichton and Livingstone-Douglas factions. After the Council of 1444 Crichton was removed as Chancellor and the office was given to Bishop Kennedy of St. Andrews, the King's uncle. Kennedy later resigned but constantly attempted to strengthen the King's position and, seeking to limit the power of Douglas, he allied himself to Crichton. Together they held the balance of power against the other party during the remainder of James' minority.

By 1448 however two new factors began to influence events. The King was growing up, he was now eighteen years old, and the truce with England was running out. The minority of Henry VI had ended but the young King of England had proved to be quite ineffective and his country suffered from similar problems to those experienced in Scotland during Royal minorities. The nobility had become overpowerful. The stage was set for the resumption of the wars of the Roses and, as the truce expired, hostilities were renewed along the border. Nothing of major significance was achieved. Dunbar and Dumfries were burned in

Scotland and Warkworth and Alnwick suffered a similar fate before a new truce was ratified. Shortly before these actions, in December of 1448, the Franco Scottish Alliance was renewed. Proposals were made to ratify it by the King's marriage, and desiring to further their trade with the continent, the Scots wished for a match with a princess of the house of Burgundy, Gueldres or Cleves. Charles VII, of France, was equally pleased at the possibility of a marriage which would bring Burgundy into the Franco-Scottish alliance and suggested that James should marry Mary, daughter of the Duke of Gueldres and niece of the Duke of Burgundy. The match was agreed. Philip of Burgundy provided a handsome dowry of 60,000 crowns and put his name to a treaty of perpetual friendship and peace. On 3rd July, 1449, James and Mary were married in splendour at Holyrood palace.

Soon after his marriage the nineteen year old King began to act as ruler in his own right. He was a strong and forceful monarch and by the end of his relatively brief personal reign he had succeeded in restoring civil order and had brought the nobility into total obedience to the Crown. He gave his country peace from the fractional squabbles of his minority and for this he was well loved. His first action was to renew the truce with England and, as soon as this had been accomplished, he utterly destroyed the power of the Livingstones. In September 1449 he arrested most of the family and charged them with "crimes comitit agaynis the King or . . . his derrest moder". Livingstone's ally, Douglas, appears to have concluded a pact of mutual aid with John of the Isles around this time but, when he was sent at the head of a Scots delegation to the Papal Jubilee, he went without protest leaving his lands in the care of his youngest brother, John of Balvenie. Crichton was taken back into the King's favour and served him loyally thereafter. With the support of the Church and the burgesses James called his first parliament in 1450 and legislated against the violence which had spread during his minority. Acts were passed to ensure that justice would prevail and that none would be oppressed, not even "the pure pepil that labouris the grunde". The work that James I had started was revived and the machinery was set up to provide firm Royal control. In the same year Scotland's second University, at Glasgow, was inaugurated and the University of St. Andrews was strengthened by Bishop Kennedy's foundation of the College of St. Salvator.

When the King had seized Livingstone and his family he had shown no antagonism towards the Earl of Douglas and he appears to have hoped for loyal service from the Earl he had admired in his youth. However, during Douglas' absence at the Papal Jubilee, the youngest of the Douglas brothers had been either unable, or unwilling, to control the activities of his tenants. The King's peace was being fragmented and James would brook no interference with his wishes. He quickly seized and destroyed a number of Douglas strongholds and executed those who refused to swear obedience to him. In retaliation for these acts against his ally, John of the Isles descended on Inverness and Badenoch but his rebellion was quelled by speedy and vigorous action. When the Earl of Douglas himself returned to Scotland from the Papal celebrations he found the King much stronger than when he had left. Although James was displeased with the actions of those whom Douglas had left to look after his lands, he assumed, or hoped, that Douglas himself was loyal. With the exception of the earldom of Wigtown, all his lands were restored and he was generally received back into the Royal favour. However gradually the King learned of the bond with John of the Isles and of a similar pact he had concluded with the "Tiger Earl" of Crawford. There was also the matter of possibly treasonable meetings with the Duke of York which had occurred during Douglas' journey to Rome. James' attitude changed forthwith. Douglas was summoned to dine in Stirling castle and realising the danger, came only after he was granted a letter of safe conduct. The meal passed pleasantly enough but tempers rose later when the King took him aside and insisted that he immediately break off relations with Crawford and John of the Isles. Douglas' refusal set James in a fury. He retorted, "False traitor, sen you will nocht, I sall", and struck him with his dagger. The murder was completed by Patrick Gray, the captain of the guard who, "strak him next efter the King with ane poleaxe on the heid and strak out his brains".

James was immediately conscience stricken over his passionate and dangerous act but had no time to rest as the Douglas family rose in rebellion. Stirling was put to the torch by the Bishop of Aberdeen who inherited the Earldom from his brother to become the ninth Earl. Crawford led a rebellion in the North but James acted with vigour and, with assistance and support from loyal nobles, both were defeated. James himself took the field against the new Earl who surrendered in the face of an immensely superior Royal army. Throughout the rebellion, which was crushed in a matter of months, the King enjoyed the wholehearted support of the Estates which exonerated him of the murder on the grounds of the late Earl's refusal to repudiate his treasonable alliances.

Remarkable clemency, probably caused by remorse, was shown to the ninth Earl. He was pardoned for his part in the rebellion, was granted the Earldom of Wigtown, given permission to marry his brother's widow and was sent to England as the prestigious head of a Scottish embassy. However James was not unaware of the possibility of further trouble. Two years after the rebellion, in 1454, Henry VI succumbed to the madness hereditary in his mother's family. The Duke of York was made protector and Douglas appears to have renewed the intrigues which had partly resulted in the downfall of the previous Earl. James received news of his dealings with York and determined to make an end of the matter. He raised an army in the spring of 1455 and marched into the Douglas lands, burning and plundering as he went. Douglas raised all his forces against him but many deserted when the King offered mercy. The ninth Earl fled to the Isles and then to England and his three brothers made a stand at Langholm where they were totally defeated. One brother was killed and one captured but the third, John of Balvenie, escaped south of the border. John of the Isles raised five thousand men under his kinsman Donald Balloch, but his raid on the west coast was repulsed. The Royal victories were followed by the condemnation of the two surviving brothers and their mother as traitors. The power of the Black Douglas was broken for good.

In the remaining five years of his reign there was peace between the King and his barons. The King and the country were both stronger than they had been since the days of Bruce, and with a respite from the internal problems which had dogged his minority and continued until Douglas was brought down, James worked to secure his gains. The parliament of 1455 attached large areas of land and strategic castles to the crown because, "the poverte of the crowne is oftymes the cause of the poverte of the Realme and mony uthir inconvenientis". James was made to swear that these lands would never be given away so that the great lords could no longer acquire a greater land holding than the King himself. Royal justice was strengthened. The powers of the Wardens of the Marches, who policed the border, were reduced and no Regalities were to be created without the consent of Parliament. Justice was strengthened and was made available to the common people of the country by the creation of a small debtors court.

Following parliaments passed legislation to strengthen the Kingdom. Able bodied men were to maintain armour and weapons according to their means. Encouragement was given to ensure that archers would be proficient with the bow and idlers who insisted on wasting time at "the fut ball and the golf" were discouraged by the imposition of fines. These pastimes were to be "uttirly cryit downe and nat uset". Artillery had become more common since James I introduced the first cannon to Scotland and certain lords were required to provide "cartis of weir (carts of war)" capable of transplanting the guns. The southern defenses were strengthened by the requirement that all able bodied men were to be required to march south if Scotland was attacked. Garrisons were set up along the border and the fords were to be watched. Arrangements were made to construct signal beacons which could be lit to give warning of advancing enemies.

Much of this legislation revived the customs which had been initiated by James I but the defensive arrangements on the border became necessary after the King wrote to Henry VI to complain about the gracious reception Douglas had received when he fled to England. Henry had always been reasonably amicably disposed towards Scotland but the letter arrived during one of his mental breakdowns and was answered by the belligerent Duke of York. York ignored James' protest and instead raised the old English claim to the overlordship of Scotland. James was informed that "we mean strongly to repress and severely punish your Insolence, Rebellion, Arrogance and rash attacks". Furious at these insults James led a Scottish force over the border in the Autumn of 1456 but, when Henry recovered and York was displaced, he withdrew and offered a two year truce which was concluded in July 1457.

Two years later, when the families of Lancaster (Henry VI) and York were contending for the throne in open battle, James prepared to enter the war on the side of the Lancastrians. There is little doubt that he preferred Henry to York but he was also prompted by the desire to recover Berwick and Roxburgh which were still in English hands. Following the battle of Northampton in July 1460, in which the Royal forces were defeated and Henry VI was captured, James gathered a large army from all parts of Scotland, and led it south to besiege Roxburgh castle. The artillery was brought up and, on the 3rd August, the King, "mair curieous nor becam him" stood by to watch the firing of a Flemish cannon owned by his father. As the powder ignited, the gun burst and James, only a few months short of his thirtieth birthday, was killed in the explosion. While his body was being taken back to Holyrood for burial, Queen Mary hastened south with her eldest son to stiffen the resolve of the besieging army. The siege was successful and Roxburgh was regained.

James III
Born May 1452
Reigned: 1460-1488
Eldest surviving son of James II
Married Princess Margaret, daughter of King Christian I of
Denmark, Norway and Sweden.
Three sons
Contemporary of:
Henry VI 1422-1461 and 1470-1471
Edward IV 1461-1470 and 1471-1483
Richard III 1483-1485 (Crookback)
Henry VII 1485-1509
Died (murdered) near Stirling
Buried in Abbey of Cambuskenneth near Stirling

The minority of James III, although marked by occasional squabbles and disloyalties, did not see a return to the anarchy which had existed during the early years of his father's reign. Mary of Gueldres, the young king's mother, assumed the role of Regent although she was never formally styled as such. It was decided merely that James "suld ay remane with the quene". She became his Guardian and was assisted by the Bishops of Glasgow and St. Andrews and by the Earls of Angus, Huntly, Argyll and Orkney. No overwhelmingly powerful noble families existed to challenge her rule and the first problems she faced originated with the Civil War which was flourishing south of the border.

Following the defeat and capture of Henry VI at Northampton, the Duke of York was named as his heir. Henry's Queen, Margaret of Anjou, hurried to Dumfries to beg assistance from the Scots. The two Queens met on amicable terms and, "remanit thar togidder X or XII days". Before their negotiations had been completed the meeting was interrupted by news of the Lancastrian victory at Wakefield and the death of the Duke of York. Margaret hurried south with an army of, "Scots, Welsh and other strangers and Northmen", but, despite achieving victory at St. Albans in February of 1461 she failed to occupy London. Edward, son of the late Duke of York, was proclaimed King Edward IV in early March and, later in the same month, defeated the Lancastrians in a snowstorm at Towton. Margaret, Henry and their son again fled to Scotland. Once more they were graciously received but, before Queen Mary promised assistance, they were constrained to surrender Berwick from English control.

Edward IV reacted to these intrigues between the Scots and Lancastrians with diplomatic ventures which were designed to occupy the Scottish government and prevent further support for the deposed Henry. The Earl of Douglas, who had rebelled against James II, was still in England and Edward drew into his scheme John, Lord of the Isles and his cousin Donald Balloch. The Isles had rendered only loose obedience to the Scottish crown from the time of Bruce and their Lords had consistently sought to make the most of any advantage which could be wrested from troubles of the central government. In 1462 the three conspirators entered into an agreement with Edward whereby they would assist him in any war against their King on the assurance that, if Edward was successful, Scotland would be partitioned among them to rule as vassals of the English King. If Edward hoped to embarrass the Scots by these moves, he certainly succeeded. With the aid of Balloch, the Lord of the Isles installed himself at Inverness where he, "tuke the Kingis fermes and all vittalis of the Kingis". He was not reconciled to James until 1464. At about the same time Douglas led a raid over the border with his brother John of Balvenie. John was captured and subsequently executed but Douglas himself escaped back to England. By this time it was becoming apparent that the red rose of Lancaster was in the eclipse. Mary began to move towards an accommodation with Edward which would have the beneficial effect of limiting the unruly acts of Douglas and John of the Isles. Her change in policy was resisted by Bishop Kennedy and the older nobles but won the support of a group of young lords who were perhaps more pragmatic and less resistant to change. However rumour suggested that her support for the Yorkists was inspired by private motives in an attempt to be revenged on the Lancastrian Duke of Somerset with whom she had an unfortunate love affair. Her name was also coupled with Adam Hepburn, the Master of Hailes, and the resulting scandal reduced her effectiveness in controlling affairs. In July 1462 the Estates separated her from the King and Bishop Kennedy took over as Regent. Later in the same year Margaret of Anjou attempted another invasion of England. She sailed to Northumberland but was forced to beat a speedy retreat to Scotland when confronted by Warwick, the Kingmaker. In the following year Margaret and Henry, together with the young King James and his mother, made another sally into England but again had to retreat at the approach of Warwick. Margaret left Scotland soon after and, when Queen Mary died at the age of 30 in December, Kennedy was left in full command. He obtained control of the young king and shortly after the signing of an Anglo-French truce, which did not include Scotland, he changed his policy and decided to come to terms with Edward IV. On 1st June 1464 a fifteen year truce was agreed and for the next ten years there was a period of relative peace between the two countries.

Bishop Kennedy died in 1465, just a few months before the King's thirteenth birthday. As James was now reaching the "perfect age" there was thought to be no need to appoint a regent to replace Kennedy. However the personal rule of such a young king merely invited a return to anarchy reminiscent of the minority of James II. Contenders for power were not lacking. Affairs of state were continued with an outward show of continuity but schemes were afoot to concentrate power in a few hands. Various bonds of alliance were forged but the chief seekers after power were the relations of the late Bishop and the adherents of Lord Boyd of Kilmarnock. Together they amounted to a formidable group. Lord Kennedy, the Bishop's brother was the Keeper of Stirling Castle whereas Lord Boyd's brother was the keeper of Edinburgh Castle and the King's military tutor. The ramification of the alliances spread far beyond the Boyds and the Kennedys but were never aimed at the person of the King and were intended rather to obtain the maximum power possible from the Royal minority. In July of 1466 Lord Boyd acted to ensure his own prominence. During a hunting expedition he abducted the young King and carried him off to Edinburgh Castle where, although he was treated graciously, he remained, in effect, a prisoner. In October Parliament met in Edinburgh and James was 'persuaded' to declare that he had accompanied Boyd of his own free will. At the same time the King announced his desire to have Lord Boyd continue as his guardian until he, James, reached the age of twenty-one. Boyd's son was quickly married to the King's sister although her marriage abroad might have been useful in establishing more solid ties with the continent. James is reported to have been furious and to have wept with anger at this shameful match for a Scots princess.

The Parliament of 1466 also empowered a commission of Lords to deal with the old question of the annual payments to Norway. These payments had been established when the western Isles were ceded to Scotland in 1266 during the reign of Alexander III and, although Bruce had confirmed the payments in 1312, the "annuale of Norway" had not been delivered since 1426. The result of the negotiations was a treaty signed in 1466 whereby James was betrothed to Margaret, daughter of King Christian I of Norway, Denmark and Sweden. James agreed to confer on his bride one third of the Royal revenues, the palace of Linlithgow and the castle of Doune but in return the Scots were to receive a dowry of 60,000 Rhenish Florins and a cancellation of annual payments and all arrears. Only 10,000 florins were to be paid before the marriage and, until full payment had been received, the Scots were to have all the lands and rights of the Norwegians in Orkney. However in 1469, when Margaret was due to depart from Norway, her father found himself unable to raise even the down payment on her dowry. Instead, he sent 2,000 florins and pledged his lands in Shetland as security for the remaining sum. James and Margaret were married in the Abbey of Holyrood on 13 July 1469.

King Christian was never able to redeem his pledge and, in due course, Orkney and Shetland passed to the Scottish crown.

James was now eighteen years old and his marriage signalled the effective end of his minority. The Boyds had been able to seize power only because of the absence of any powerful competitors and, with an equal absence of strong friends, they fell as quickly as they had risen. Within a month of his marriage James marched against them and by November the family had been declared guilty of treason because of their earlier abduction of the King's person. James began his personal rule by consolidating the Scottish position in Orkney. He persuaded the Scottish Earl of Orkney to exchange his lands for equivalent holdings in Fife. The earldom of Orkney and the lordship of Shetland then passed to the Crown itself and was "nocht to be gevin away".

The year of 1469 saw a resumption of the Civil War in England. Margaret of Anjou invaded England, now in conjunction with Warwick and the Duke of Clarence who had turned against Edward IV. For a short time they were successful in re-establishing Henry VI but within a year Edward was back on the throne. Because of the possibility of war with France, Edward was anxious to secure his northern border. A short Anglo-Scots truce was signed in 1471 and, in 1474, a more lasting truce of forty-five years was negotiated. However no sooner had James come to a settlement with England than he had to turn his attention once more to the Western Islands. John of the Isles had submitted to the King in 1464 but since then he had again begun to show an independence which threatened the integrity of the kingdom. James may also have learned of his treasonable relations with Douglas and Edward IV and determined at last to bring the Isles firmly under the Crown. In 1466 he annexed the earldom of Ross to the crown but succeeded in pacifying John by confirming him in possession of the rest of his lands. He was also given the title of Baron, Lord of the Isles and was made a Lord of Parliament. John seems to have sub-mitted relatively cheerfully to the Royal Authority but his illegitimate son, Angus of Islay, was less inclined to a reconciliation and kept the North in turmoil until the end of the reign. The future was, however, to see the development of much more serious problems which would culminate in open rebellion.

James was quite unlike his father. He took no pleasure in the warlike activities normal for a young man of noble birth, was relatively uninterested in administration and "delyttit mair in singing and playing upon instrumentis". He was interested in literature, painting, architecture and "desyrit never to heir of weiris (wars) nor the fame thairof". In these pursuits he was totally at variance with most of the nobility and quite different from his two brothers, the Duke of Albany and the Earl of Mar. The growing unpopularity of the King corresponded with the emergence of Albany and Mar as young vigorous statesmen in their own right. In 1478 James was sufficiently concerned about the admiration they commanded to have them imprisoned on charges that they had abused their authority. Mar's death in Edinburgh castle further injured the King's reputation which was not enhanced by Albany's spectacular escape and flight to England. Galloping inflation was fundamental to his lack of popularity but, most damaging of all, was his practice of surrounding himself with low born favourites having his own interests in music and literature and showing the same repugnance for the martial arts. When his popularity was at its lowest ebb, relations with England deteriorated. A proposal to restore the friendship of earlier years was snubbed by Edward IV who revived yet again the English claim to overlordship and suggested that the Scots give up Berwick and restore the lands of the Earl of Douglas. Belligerence increased on both sides. James sent an ultimatum informing Edward that if he did not cease to provide aid to Burgundy the Scots would intervene on behalf of their old ally. Hostilities broke out and, in the early years of the 1480's, both countries made preparations for a full scale war which was averted by Papal intervention. However, in 1482, Albany, still in England, signed an agreement at Fotheringay in which he styled himself, "King of Scotland by the gift of the King of England", and acknowledged Edward IV as his overlord. In return for promises that he would be a vassal King, Albany was given an English army and, in 1483, he and the Duke of Gloucester marched to lay siege to Berwick. James raised an army to oppose them and marched South to Lauderdale. However he took with him most of his court favourites and the feelings of the disgruntled lords broke out in sudden resentment against the King and his companions. In what appears to have been quite unpremeditated rebellion James was seized, all except one of his favourites were hanged and the army returned to Edinburgh. The King was confined to Edinburgh Castle from July to September but his personal unpopularity was not so great that open rebellion could be easily countenanced and he was released and reconciled not only to those who had seized him in Lauderdale but also to Albany. In an effort to win his brother's loyalty James made him the Lieutenant of the Kingdom but, in 1483, Albany secretly reaffirmed his earlier agreement with Edward IV. His duplicity was discovered. Dismissed from the lieutenancy in March, he fled to England. In June he was declared a traitor and his lands and goods were forfeited. Edward IV died suddenly in April and Albany received little encouragement from the new King, Richard III. In a last desperate attempt, he and Douglas invaded Scotland with a small force in 1484. Douglas was captured and sent to the Abbey of Lindores where he spent the rest of his life. Albany escaped but was accidentally killed in a tournament in France the following year.

With the eclipse of Albany and Douglas, James seemed free at last of the problems which had beset him for so long. A new Anglo-Scots truce was arranged in 1484. Henry VII's victory on Bosworth Field settled the War of the Roses and plans were made to ensure stability between the two nations by the proposed marriage of James, now a widower, to Elizabeth Woodville, the eldest daughter of Edward IV and sister in law of the new English King. The proposal came to nothing because once again James was faced by rebellion. He seems to have learnt little form the episode at Lauderdale and had heaped favours and authority on the one friend who had not been hanged. Three parliaments since then had urged him to pay more attention to the administration of his kingdom but their appeals were ignored. In 1488 the nobles rose against him, seized his eldest son, and marched through southern Scotland proclaiming the Prince as Governor of the Kingdom. James raised support from the Northern Earls and met the rebels near the river Forth where there was a minor skirmish followed by a "pacification". Within a few months the settlement fell apart and the King was once more faced by open rebellion. He again raised an army and, on 11 June 1488, the Royalists met the rebels within sight of Stirling Castle. The battle of Sauchieburn resulted in few casualties but ended with the defeat of the King's army. During his subsequent flight James was thrown from his horse and injured near a mill standing to the west of the village of Bannockburn. He was taken into the mill and asked for a priest so that he could be shriven before his enemies found him. On learning that her injured guest was the King himself the miller's wife, "clappit hir handis and ran fourth and cryit for ane priest to the King". She quickly found a man claiming to be a priest but, on returning to the mill with him, the stranger offered the King no absolution and instead "gif him four or fyve straikes ewin to the hart". The assassin's identity was never discovered.

James IV
Born March 1473
Reigned: 1488-1513
Eldest son of James III
Married Margaret Tudor, daughter of Henry VII
Four sons and two daughters by Margaret; five illegitimate children
Contemporary of:
Henry VII 1485-1509
Henry VIII 1509-1547
Died at Flodden

James IV has been described as the ideal Renaissance Prince. He had a keen and lively mind and, although he had his father's interests in the Arts, considerable time and energy were devoted to the administration of justice and to the defence of the realm. He was courageous and on some occasions foolhardy but became well loved because of his generosity to the poor and his accessibility to all people. He took considerable interest in education and was reputed to speak six foreign languages in addition to his own Scots and, "the language of the savages who live in some parts of Scotland and of the Islands". Aberdeen University was established in 1495. In the following year the first compulsory education act was passed, compelling "all barroins and freholdaris that are of substance" to send their children to school where they were to remain until they were "competentlie foundit and have perfyte latyne". The printing press, introduced to England by Caxton during the previous reign was brought to Scotland in 1508 and had far reaching effects in the spread of literature. James showed interest in the developing sciences and was instrumental in setting up the Royal College of Surgeons in Edinburgh because of his fascination with surgery and dentistry. The necessities of securing civil peace were not ignored and he revived and centralised the supreme court which had been set up by James I but which had lapsed during the reign of James III. In addition much time was spent presiding over itinerant criminal courts around the country and the King pronounced himself well satisfied when he was able to ride alone from Stirling to Elgin with no ill effects.

The death of his father after the battle at Sauchieburn caused the new King great remorse. He was only fifteen years old at the time and had probably little opportunity of resisting the rebels who had carried him off as their figure-head. Indeed, prior to the battle James had given strict instructions that his father was not to be harmed. Later, when he discovered that his orders had been ignored, his grief was so great that he declared he would not seek, and indeed would refuse, to be absolved of the crime. In penance he wound an iron chain round his waist and it remained there under the silk and gold cloth for the rest of his life.

Scotland was outraged by the assassination of James III and, although the rebel lords quickly secured positions of eminence, the feeling in the country and James' natural inclination towards generosity combined to prevent recriminations against those who had fought on the losing side. The first parliament of the reign confirmed the heirs of those who had been killed fighting for James III just as if their fathers had died peacefully in the service of the crown. Most of those who had remained loyal to James III transferred their allegiance to his son and the short rebellion which broke out in 1489 faded out from lack of popular support. After the rebellion James showed his customary leniency and tempered severity with forgiveness. The castles of the three rebel lords were razed to the ground and their lands were forfeited but, before long, James restored them to their previous positions.

The sudden and violent change in the Scottish Government caused some unease in England because Henry VII had been on friendly terms with James III who had generally attempted to keep the peace despite the contrary opinion of some of the nobility. The acts of privateers at sea increased the dangers inherent in the political situation but neither Henry VII nor James IV were in favour of renewing the hostility which had led to so much trouble in the past. Initially, however, privateering operations were unofficially sanctioned and Henry attempted to reduce the risk of war by keeping the Scots busy with the actions of malcontents whom he secretly encouraged. James IV was very much an unknown quantity at the beginning of his reign but when it became apparent that he was firmly established in power and reacted moderately to international incidents which might have led to war if handled impetuously, it seemed that there was a good chance of both nations developing peacefully. By 1491, three years after James' coronation at Scone, the international problems had been to some extent settled and a five year truce was concluded.

With the English question out of the way, James was now free to turn his attention to the Isles. The Western Isles had been a source of trouble for longer than most men could remember. In the previous reign the Lord of the Isles had rebelled on several occasions and, although he had submitted to the King in 1464, his illegitimate son, Angus, had been angered by the loss of the Earldom of Ross and kept the area in turmoil until he was assassinated in 1490. The death of Angus did not, however, see the total integration of the Isles with the rest of Scotland. Another leader appeared in the nephew of the old Lord of the Isles. The root of the problem lay in the semi autonomous independence which the Isles had constantly enjoyed since the time of Robert Bruce. James tackled the problem on two fronts. The lordship of the Isles was forfeited to the crown in 1493 and between then and 1498 James showed the Islemen the strength of the central authority by making several expeditions to their territory. At the same time he attempted, by force of personality, to persuade them to transfer their loyalty for the Lord of the Isles to the Crown and in this he was largely successful. However, as was the case with Bruce, the loyalty of the Isles was directed to James himself rather than to the institution of the Crown and the gains he had accomplished fell apart when he was killed at Flodden. There are widely varying opinions regarding his success in integrating the Isles with the rest of the country. At one extreme it has been suggested that their integration was the "outstanding achievement" of his reign whereas opposing views hold that nothing changed except that the MacDonalds became supplanted by the King's agents, the Campbells and the Gordons, who were entrusted with the problem when James became occupied with foreign affairs in 1498.

Although a truce was signed with King Henry VII in 1491 the internal problems which existed between Scotland and England had never been fully settled. There was little evidence at that time to indicate that the ruinous wars of the Roses were really over and, as the English still held Berwick — captured by the Duke of Gloucester during the first rebellion against James III — the Scots were not loth to take advantage of anything which might embarrass the English King. Accordingly, when a pretender, Perkin Warbeck, arrived in Scotland in 1495, he was most graciously treated. Warbeck claimed to be Richard, Duke of York, the younger of Edward IV's two sons who had been imprisoned (and murdered?) in the tower. He had already been recognised by the Duchess of York, Edward IV's sister and by Maximillian who would become Emperor of the Holy Roman Empire. Whether James believed Warbeck's claim or not it suited his policy to take up the cause. Soon after he arrived in Scotland Warbeck was married amid great splendour to the daughter of the Earl of Huntly. A yearly allowance was allotted to him so that he might establish himself as befitted a prince of England and James prepared to go to war on his behalf.

In September of 1496 the army of James, King of Scotland, and Richard, "King of England" crossed the Tweed and invited "King Richard's" subjects to rally to his support. This they refused to do and when Warbeck would not permit the Scots army to recoup their expenses by plundering, "his subjects", the expedition retired to Scotland. Another equally inconclusive expedition was mounted in the following year but the possibility of war was removed when the English captured Warbeck during his attempt to invade Cornwall.

Henry VII now eagerly desired peace with his truculent northern neighbour. In 1498 the proposal was made that a lasting peace might be achieved by the marriage of James to Henry's daughter Margaret Tudor. Lengthy negotiations took place and, with no insuperable obstacles to the matter, these were successfully concluded in 1502 by the signing of a marriage treaty which included clauses to convert the truce into "perpetual peace". Prior to his marriage James had several mistresses which was, in the fifteenth century, quite acceptable for a young unmarried but virile monarch. Of these, the King had become deeply attached to Margaret Drummond and this might have caused difficulties had she not died in 1500. The circumstances of her death were suspicious. She and her two sisters appear to have died of food poisoning but there were grave suspicions of murder and the King was quite distraught. Nevertheless Margaret's death removed any personal objections to the match and James and Margaret Tudor were married on the 8th August 1503 in the Abbey of Holyrood. The bride wore a crown made from eighty-three gold coins and, although she could not be described as beautiful, she made a striking figure with her long red hair reaching down to the ground. James was dressed in, "a robe of white damask figured with gold, a jacket with slashes of crimson satin and the border of black velvet, a waistcoat of cloth of gold, and a pair of scarlet hose".

By the time of the King's marriage Scotland was prospering. The civil disturbances of the previous reign had virtually disappeared and the wealthy landowners, following the example of their King, were "giving their whole minds to the arts of peace". Indeed six years before his marriage a Spanish ambassador had written that there was "as great a difference between the Scotland of old time and the Scotland of today as there is between bad and good". James must have felt satisfaction as he surveyed the results of his efforts over the last fifteen years. He had rooted out the troublemakers and given the poorer people security from the deprivations caused by the squabbling of the nobility; a security which rested solidly on the courts and the King's peace. Literature, education, trade and commerce were flourishing and the country was at last in a state of "perpetual peace" with England.

He now turned his attention to the international scene. His diplomatic success in achieving peace with England without losing the friendship of France gave him the aura of a European statesman and his services as a mediator in continental affairs were employed on several occasions. Partly to satisfy his own ego and partly to further his ambitions to raise Scotland to the rank of a leading European nation, he determined to build a navy. It would be used to protect the Scottish shoreline and to suppress piracy but, perhaps most important, it would lend credibility to James' desire for a grand crusade against the Turks.

The events which eventually embroiled Scotland in another war with England began around 1508 in Italy. In an attempt to extend the secular control of the papacy, Pope Julius II united with France and the Emperor Maximillian in a league against Venice. England joined the league at the end of the year but, when Venice was defeated, Julius completely reversed his policy in order to oust the French who had been altogether too successful and had overrun most of northern Italy. In 1511 a "Holy League" was formed. Spain, Venice, England and the Emperor were now allied against Louis, and the dangers to France and her ally Scotland were obvious. James resorted to diplomacy in an effort to resolve the dispute but was unsuccessful. The situation became critical because events in England had resulted in a deterioration of the friendly relationship which had been cultivated under Henry VII. Henry died in 1509 and was succeeded by his son Henry VIII who was much more aggressive than his father and much less inclined to use diplomatic means of solving what, in themselves, were relatively minor incidents between the Scots and the English. Henry was also eager to revive his ancestors' achievements on the continent and France began to put pressure on Scotland to ensure her support in the coming struggle. Early in 1512 James was told that the French supported his conception of a crusade against the Turks and that considerable aid would be forthcoming as soon as Pope

Julius and the Holy League made peace. In April he was informed that the French would support any rightful claim to the English throne and, in July, torn between what was perceived as the true and tested friendship of France and the growing belligerence of England, the Franco-Scottish treaty was renewed. Both countries bound themselves to make full scale war on England if either were attacked. In April of the following year Henry VIII signed the Treaty of Malines with the Emperor. This document virtually committed both to make war on France and, in June, Henry sailed from England to supervise the invasion. Just prior to his departure, envoys from France arrived in Scotland bearing letters from King Louis and his Queen. In a typical medieval gesture Queen Anne sent a ring to James with the request that he be her knight and come to her aid by advancing into England. Henry's invasion of France made it virtually certain that Scotland would enter the war. James sent him an ultimatum in late July and the answer he received removed any doubts that he had been correct in choosing to support the old friendship with France in preference to the rather shaky alliance with England. His envoys to the English were instructed to carry word back to James saying that Henry was "the very owner of Scotland" and that on his return from France he would expel "the vassal (who) doth rebel against me". War was declared and the Scottish fleet was dispatched to the continent carrying artillery and, unfortunately, the best of the Scottish gunners. Hostilities broke out in early August with an "ill raid" on Northumberland and by the 22nd of the month the Scots army was over the Tweed. Four castles had been captured by the first week in September when James moved his men into a strong defensive position on Flodden Hill, on the western bank of the River Till, to await the approach of the Earl of Surrey and the English army. When Surrey arrived at Alnwick, about 20 miles from the Scots encampment, he sent James a formal challenge to a pitched engagement coupled with a chivalric appeal that it would be more fitting to fight on the open plain to the south. James was not impressed by the suggestion that he should leave his strong position and refused to see Surrey's messenger, contenting himself by replying that he, "would hold his ground at his own pleasure", and would wait for Surrey until noon on the 9th September. The English marched north along the Eastern bank of the Till, out of range of the Scottish guns, and on the morning of the 9th they crossed the river at a point five miles north of the Scottish position. The move took the Scots by surprise. They had been facing south and had to hurriedly make new plans to face the English army which now lay between them and Scotland. Quickly they marched the short distance from Flodden to Branxton Hill to ensure that Surrey would not gain the high ground. This was still a strong defensive position but had the added advantage that, if Surrey chose to ignore his challenge and march into Scotland, the army of the King would be in a better position to come to grips with him. The battle opened with a decisive artillery duel. Although James had the larger cannon Surrey had more of them and it is probable that, during the hurried move from Flodden to Branxton, the Scots had been unable to rearrange all their guns. Whereas the most experienced Scots gunners had been sent to France with the fleet, the English employed expert German gunners who soon found the range and put the Scottish artillery out of action. The ensuing bombardment forced the Scots to leave their position and attack. At four o'clock in the afternoon the Scottish spearmen charged down the hill, having taken their shoes off to retain a better grip on the slippery wet ground. At close quarters their fifteen foot spears were no match for the shorter English halberds. James, leading the centre battalion, fought through the English ranks to within a spear's length of Surrey before he was killed. The hand to hand fighting could have only one result. By nightfall Surrey had achieved outright victory. In addition to the King and his illegitimate son Alexander, the dead numbered "two bishops, three abbots, one dean, nine earls, fourteen lords, and three highland chiefs". English claims indicated ten thousand Scottish dead, almost half the army.

After the battle, James' body was conveyed to Richmond but was never given the state funeral which Henry VIII had planned. It is said to have remained, wrapped in lead, at the monastery of Skene in Surrey until the reign of Elizabeth I when a workman cut off the head because of the pleasant smell of the embalming spices. At a later date the head was interred in the charnel house of the Church of St. Michael's in Wood St. but the fate of the headless body is unknown. In Scotland the people refused to believe that their King was dead. He was believed to have survived the battle and to have journeyed to Jerusalem from where he would return to rule again.

James V
Born 1512
Reigned: 1513-1542
Eldest surviving son of James IV
Married:
(1) Princes Madeleine, daughter of Francis I
(2) Marie of Guise Lorraine, widow of Duc de Longueville
Two sons and one daughter by Marie, seven illegitimate sons
Contemporary of Henry VIII 1509-1547
Died at Falkland, Fife
Buried at Holyrood, Edinburgh

When James IV died at Flodden, his son and heir, also James, was less than two years old. Prior to leaving home at the head of the Scottish troops the King had made a will naming Queen Margaret the young boy's guardian. She must have realised the dangers inherent in the succession of yet another minor and, when news of the disaster reached her at Linlithgow, she had little time to mourn her husband. Within twelve days of the King's death, James V was crowned at the "Mourning Coronation" in Stirling. Margaret duly assumed office at the head of the Scottish Government and a Council of Regency was appointed to advise her. But Margaret was a woman, and even worse, was the sister of Henry VIII, King of the nation which had so recently inflicted a devastating defeat on the Scots. Only a short time before the battle Henry had claimed to be overlord of Scotland. Afterwards he did not press the claim but wanted to be recognised as the, "Protector of Scotland", because of his close relationship to James, his nephew, and to the Queen, his sister. In view of these strong family ties it is not surprising that Margaret's appointment was opposed When her husband was killed the nearest male to the throne after James V was John Stewart, the Duke of Albany. Albany was the son of James III's brother Alexander who had fled to France after the unsuccessful rebellion of 1484. Despite his suspicious heredity Albany was well known to the Scottish nobility. He had corresponded with James IV and, on occasions, had assisted him with negotiations in France where he was well respected as an Admiral of France and a friend of Francis I. The death of James IV made Albany heir presumptive, the natural, and traditional, choice for the Regency. A movement favouring his appointment grew and before the end of 1513 a preliminary letter had been sent requesting his assistance during the King's minority.

Margaret had been pregnant when she was widowed at Flodden. Although her condition gained much sympathy she became less able to attend to affairs of state as the birth of her child approached. A son was born in April and, before the baby was seven months old, she shocked the country by marrying the Earl of Angus, head of the powerful Douglas family. It is quite probable that at this time she felt in need of support from a strong man who commanded a powerful following in the country but it was commonly believed that Margaret had married "for her plesour". Although the marriage was performed secretly there was no possibility that the news should be kept quiet. When they learned of her action the Albany faction were overjoyed because the terms of James IV's will appointed her as Guardian only for as long as she did not remarry. When this was brought to her notice she had no other choice than to resign and agree to Albany's appointment to the Regency.

Albany arrived in Scotland in May of 1515 and was

installed as Regent in ceremonies performed in Edinburgh at the beginning of July. Realising that possession of the King's person was critical, he demanded that Margaret hand over James into his custody. The Queen refused and continued to do so until the Regent appeared before Stirling Castle with over 7000 men and the great cannon, Mons Meg, the largest artillery piece in Scotland. Reluctantly she surrendered the keys of the castle together with the three year old King and his younger brother, born after her confinement of the previous year. The Royal children remained at Stirling while Albany set up in residence at Holyrood. Margaret was escorted to Edinburgh castle. She did not see the King again for over two years and was never reunited with her youngest child.

Shortly after leaving her children, Margaret, now pregnant by Angus, fled from Edinburgh and joined her husband. He had been with her when Albany first demanded custody of the King but, finding his advice to give up James ignored, he had fled from Stirling before any trouble broke out. Together they journeyed south to Northumberland where Margaret gave birth to a daughter destined to become the mother of Lord Darnley, husband to Mary Queen of Scots.

With Margaret and Angus both out of Scotland, the Regent began to consolidate his position. Lord Home, who was known to have assisted the Queen with her escape plans, was arrested and placed in the custody of the Earl of Arran. However, within a short time of his arrest, Home persuaded Arran to join with him in a rising against Albany. They were joined by Angus but the plot was upset by speedy and vigorous action by the Regent. The rebellion was broken before it had begun. Angus fled back to England but abandoned his wife for the second time and returned to Scotland when Albany offered clemency. Henry VIII's comment on learning of this treatment of his sister was, "Done like a Scot". Although the three principals received pardons for their misdeeds, Home was later discovered to have continued plotting and to have contracted treasonable negotiations with England after his release. In the late Autumn of 1516 both he and his brother were executed. Shortly afterwards Albany was officially recognised as heir presumptive and in April of the following year he journeyed to France, partly to attend to Franco-Scottish affairs, but also to take care of personal matters which had arisen during his two years in Scotland.

Although he had not intended to depart for long, the Regent was unable to return to Scotland until four years had passed. While he was in France, the French King, Francis I, settled his differences with Henry VIII and was persuaded to keep Albany out of Scotland so that Henry's sister, Margaret, might have the opportunity to regain her former position as head of State.

During his sojourn Albany negotiated the Treaty of Rouen by which James V was eventually married, albeit by a circuitous route, to Princess Madeleine, Francis I's third daughter. In Scotland his absence provoked a return to the type of problem which had become commonplace during royal minorities. Margaret returned to Scotland soon after Albany's departure and she and Angus set up in opposition to the Earl of Arran who was in nominal control during the Regent's absence. In addition to a long standing rivalry between the house of Douglas, led by Angus, and the Hamilton family, led by Arran, there was friction because of their differing political views. Arran supported Albany and the French alliance whereas Angus, married to the sister of Henry VIII, wished for a settlement with England. The antagonism between these two equally powerful nobles led to violence which culminated in a street battle in Edinburgh during 1520 when the Hamiltons were driven out of the city. Had Margaret and Angus acted with unity the English party might have gained the ascendancy but Margaret had become quite disillusioned with her husband. There were financial problems. Angus was known to have taken a mistress while his wife was in England and she had probably not forgiven him for deserting her to make common cause with Albany in 1516. In 1519 she was contemplating divorce but was discouraged by her brother's attitude and, when Albany returned to Scotland in 1521, he found that Margaret had reversed her previous policy to become one of his most ardent supporters. Probably she hoped that Albany would intercede for her with the Pope and would be able to procure the divorce she wanted. The sudden friendship between two former enemies led inevitably to scandal and rumours which suggested that more than politics was involved. Henry VIII accused Albany of seducing his sister and warned the Estates that if they did not expel the Regent, England would not renew the truce which was due to expire in January 1522.

By the time Henry's demands were made known Albany and his supporters had managed to reduce the influence of Angus and the pro-English faction. The Scots were reluctant to lose the Regent who had given them better government than had been experienced during his enforced absence and, rather than accede to Henry's ultimatum, they made ready for the expiry of the truce by preparing for war.

Albany had only been permitted to return to Scotland when the rather shaky Anglo-French alliance collapsed after Francis I and Henry VIII met at the "Field of the Cloth of Gold". In 1521 English forces raided the north of France. The attack on their ally, irritation with Henry's dictatorial attitude and fear of English antagonism led to Scottish preparations for an invasion of England. Albany led his forces south in the Autumn but, on reaching the border, the Scots lords refused to go any further. In a letter to France the Regent later explained that the nobles complained because Scotland had never benefited from the wars with England and that recent military actions had all been undertaken in the interests of France alone. No doubt they remembered only too vividly the disaster of Flodden which had crowned their last effort on behalf of France. With the Scots lords adamant a temporary truce was declared. As it had now become obvious that Scotland would not attack without more than moral encouragement from their ally, Albany returned to France to seek military support. Following his departure Henry again tried to persuade the Estates to remove him from the Regency. As an inducement he offered his daughter (Bloody) Mary as a fitting wife for the young Scots King. He also stated his readiness to sign a protracted truce if Scotland refused to take Albany back but, when the Estates spurned his proposals, which they deeply distrusted, he resorted to force and sent an army to ravage the south of Scotland.

Henry's army was led by the son of, "old Surrey", victor of Flodden. Kelso and Jedburgh were both destroyed and set on fire and it was said that, "neither house, fortress, village, tree, cattle, corn nor other succour for man", were left in the wake of the English army. Albany returned to Scotland on the very day on which Jedburgh went up in flames. With him he brought 4000 infantry supported by horses and guns. The cost of maintaining this force and the recent English success necessitated an immediate reprisal even though it was late in the year for a military campaign. Once again the Scots army marched south and once again, despite the presence of the French, the nobility was unwilling to cross into England. Finally they were persuaded to ford the Tweed but an inconclusive attack on Wark castle, the low morale and the approach of a strong English army, forced Albany to withdraw. Realising that he could do little more, the French troops were sent home and Albany, himself, sailed for France in May 1524. He promised to return by the end of August on pain of forfeiting the Regency but, within a few months, he had been superseded by his old rival, Margaret. With Albany out of Scotland and Angus still in France, where he had been banished after the fracas in Edinburgh, Margaret approached the Earl of Arran. Together they decided to make a bid for power. James was now twelve years old and ready, so they declared, to rule in his own right. In July 1524 he was brought from Stirling and invested with the sword, sceptre and crown of state. The Regency was declared to be terminated. Albany's supporters were imprisoned or quelled by a show of force and Margaret and Arran were left in full control.

Now that Margaret had achieved the power she had

sought for so long, the English party quickly established itself as the dominant group. However in June, one month prior to the "erection" of the King, the Earl of Angus had arrived in London and in October he returned to Scotland. He also favoured an English alliance and in February of 1525 parliament restored everything he had lost when banished. In March he was formally reconciled with his wife and became a member of her Council over which he quickly established his authority. But the formal reconciliation was quite superficial. Enmity between the two again surfaced and before long Margaret had obtained a divorce. Division within the English group became so pronounced that, in July, it was agreed that custody of the King should rotate among four Lords, the idea being that James should "keep company" with each for a quarter of the year. Angus' subsequent bid for power was devastatingly simple. He obtained custody of James for the first quarter but, in November, when the three months were completed, Angus, "would in no wise part with him". Having possession of the King's person provided the opportunity to establish the Douglas family as the premier authority in Scotland. Margaret and Arran declared these actions to be treason but the young King was constrained to write to his mother and tell her that he remained with the Earl of Angus, "cheerfully, willingly and contentedly". In a private and secretly written letter, however, he made known his real feelings, imploring her to set him free and, "to accomplish it by main force of arms", if necessary.

Supported by a number of Lords and Bishops, Margaret and Arran marched on Edinburgh but were foiled when Angus brought the King out of town at the head of a large body of his supporters. Fearing that a set battle would result in James being injured, or killed, Margaret's force retreated and dispersed. The confrontation signalled the pattern of future events. Concern for the King's safety inhibited those who might have opposed Angus and, with virtually no opposition, he was able to establish his relatives in all the important offices of state. When Margaret married for the third time in 1526 she chose the Captain of her Guard for a husband. This poor match for a former Queen so disgusted the Earl of Arran that he decided to abandon Margaret's cause. Shortly afterwards he took the opportunity to join up with Angus.

For the next two years Angus was the virtual ruler of Scotland. His authority was solidly based on possession of the King and Angus made sure that he was closely watched. Nevertheless, the humiliation that James suffered by the constant supervison became known and on three different occasions efforts were made to overthrow Angus by force. The attempts failed but James developed a deep and abiding hatred for his jailor and for the whole Douglas family, a hatred which was not alleviated by Angus' attempts to distract him with fine clothes, women and an abundance of money.

In the spring of 1528 the King escaped and rode to Stirling where he was joined by his mother and a number of loyal lords. The power of the Douglas family was quickly broken. Previously Angus had been able to direct James' public utterances but, now that the King was free, all control was gone. James forbade Angus to approach within six miles of him and, when the Estates met in September, Angus was condemned for treason, "in holding of our sovereign lord's person against his will . . . and in exposing of his person to battle . . . for which causes they have forfeited their lives, lands and goods". The Earl had taken refuge at the castle of Tantallon and, after the pronouncement of parliament, James attempted to reduce the castle by siege with, "bronze guns and powder". The affair was a humiliating failure but, after the Earl of Argyll, with his extensive military experience, took command of the siege, Angus was forced to surrender. When he did so, in November, it was on condition that he would be allowed to depart to 'England with those of his family who wished to accompany him. He never returned to Scotland while James lived.

Having been chief of the English party during the King's minority, Angus was warmly welcomed by Henry VIII. But the King of England had already set out on the long and difficult task of divorcing Catherine of Aragon and he had no wish to use Angus' banishment as an excuse for renewing hostilities while the divorce negotiations were proceeding. He did, indeed, make a formal protest but the divorce occupied most of his time and, in December of 1528 a five years peace was agreed between the two countries. This peace, and Angus' exile, at last left James to be master of his own country.

James reigned until December 1542. He was the last Catholic King of Scotland and was admired by the early historians, partly because of the contrast between his actions and those of his widow and daughter who followed him to power. His efforts to make the countryside safe from thieves and vagabonds endeared him to his poorer subjects and his popularity was enhanced by his habit of wandering abroad disguised as a poor farmer, "the Gudeman of Ballengeich". Nevertheless there was a darker side to his character which became particularly obvious towards the end of his reign. His severity in dealing with fractious members of the nobility at times verged into rapicity and the forfeiture of their lands was often governed more by greed than by a just desire to punish. The excesses which Angus had encouraged, in an attempt to distract his attention from captivity, developed a certain degree of licentiousness. Knox described him as being, "called by some a good poor man's king; of others he was termed a murderer of the nobility and one that had decreed their whole destruction. Some praised him for the repressing of theft and oppression; others dispraised him for the defouling of men's wives and virgins. . . . And yet none spoke altogether beside the truth; for . . . as the virtues could not be denied, so could not the vices by any craft be cloaked".

By birth James was half Tudor and his heredity has been blamed, perhaps too strongly, for the destructive traits which eventually alienated him from the nobility. These black aspects of his character have been described as combining to give him, "the acquisitiveness of his grandfather Henry VII, the lust and ruthlessness of his uncle Henry VIII and the unrelenting cruelty of his cousin, Bloody Mary".

At the beginning of the period of his personal reign, James gave little indication of these flaws in his character. With the Douglas family out of the way he introduced loyal supporters to the chief administrative posts but did not hesitate to retain experienced administrators whose loyalty had been to the government rather than to Angus. Soon he turned his attention to the problems of law and order and dealt with the two perennial trouble spots, the Isles and the borders. In November of 1528, even before he had dealt finally with Angus, "Letters of Fire and Sword", were issued against the disorderly Clan Chattan which was to be totally exterminated, sparing only priests, women and children who were to be deported to Shetland and Norway. There is some doubt whether his orders were implemented but there is no doubt that, in the following year he marched to the borders for the purpose, as he carefully explained to Henry VIII, of putting, "good order and rule upon them and to staunch the thefts and robberies committed by thieves and traitors". The border expedition was successful in capturing and executing two notorious robbers but the example had little effect and he returned in March 1530 to arrest and hang several others. The second visit, just over a year after the first, had the desired result and the borders remained quiet, if not contented, during the remainder of his reign.

By 1530 however there were other pressing problems. The years of James' minority had seen a tremendous reduction in the Royal revenues, from over £30,000 per year during the reign of James IV to about £13,000 in 1526. Four years later the problems were so severe that the King was reduced to borrowing from the Earl of Huntly. The difficulties were tackled on two fronts.

In 1531 James approached the Pope for a subsidy of £10,000 a year, "for the protection and defence of the realm". The amount requested was enormous but the political situation was favourable because heresy was spreading and

England was defying Rome over the matter of Henry's divorce from Catherine of Aragon. The Pope temporised in the face of his huge demand but then granted James a tenth of the annual income of the Church for three years. However it was felt that improvement in law and order would help to stop the infiltration of heresy which was rampant in England at that time and in 1531, a Bull was issued authorising a subsidy of £10,000 a year for as long as the King of Scotland remained true to the Roman faith. This was to be used to set up a Scottish College of Justice. The Scottish clergy were aware of the King's financial needs but found £10,000 a year just too much to raise. Instead they came to an agreement that, instead of the annual subsidy, they would pay £1,400 a year in perpetuity and a lump suum of £72,000 over a period of four years. Parliament ratified the institution of a College of Justice in 1541. It was to consist of fifteen judges including the president, and would provide Scotland, for the first time, with a paid judiciary. However, although the College was sorely needed, its establishment was, to a large extent, a financial expedient to lessen the poverty of the Crown. In the event the annual subsidy of £1,400 was inadequate and money had to be raised from other sources.

By 1531, in spite of the financial problems he faced, James was a very eligible bachelor. European politics were confused and Scotland was courted in high places. Over the next three years James was presented with the Golden Fleece by the Emperor, the Garter by Henry VIII and the order of St. Michael by the King of France. Each of these Monarchs suggested brides for the King who saw marriage as another way of solving his financial problems. After a number of abortive negotiations he finally made his decision and, on 1 January 1537, he was married to Madeleine, the eldest surviving daughter of Francis I. Her dowry consisted of 100,000 livres and the income from another 125,000 livres. Madeleine never enjoyed good health and, when she died only eighteen weeks after her wedding, James again looked to France for a bride. Within a year he was again married, to Marie of Guise-Lorraine, the eldest daughter of the Duke of Guise.

Marriage negotiations and monetary problems did not detract from James' efforts to secure order within his realm. He had largely settled the border problem in 1530 but there were still problems in the Isles. During the previous reign James IV had entrusted the Campbells of Argyll with maintaining order in this westerly trouble spot. However the actions of the Earl of Argyll in furthering his own interests had led to a gathering of the MacDonalds of Islay and the MacLeans of Duart. In 1531, James prepared to lead an army north to deal with them. However the chiefs came to him voluntarily with their complaints against Argyll. These were recognised to be just and, instead of taking his army against the MacDonalds, James deprived Argyll of his office and placed him in prison. For the rest of his reign there was no more trouble in the Southern Isles although, further north, there was an abortive attempt on the part of the MacDonalds of Skye and the MacLeods of Lewis to regain the Earldom of Ross. Throughout the 1530's the King acted with vigour against those who opposed his will. In doing so he brought order to the land but greatly alienated the nobility until it was said in 1537 that, "so save a dread King and so ill beloved of his subjects (the nobility) was never in this land".

The years following his marriage were years in which James reached the pinnacle of his power. Scotland was at peace with its neighbours and order prevailed at home. Two sons were born within three years of his marriage and the Royal finances were thriving. Money was available for non essentials and there was a flowering of Renaissance splendour. The palace of Holyrood was extended and an ambitious architectural programme resulted in the construction of new, and the modernisation of existing, Royal palaces. A new crown, still to be seen in Edinburgh castle, was completed in 1542 and there can be little doubt that James was more deserving of the description of a Renaissance Prince than was his father or grandfather. Then it all began to fall apart. The two Princes both died in 1541 and international dangers arose with Henry VIII's excommunication and the possibility of war between England and the

European powers which remained faithful to Rome. Henry began to put his defences in order. The south coast was strengthened to repel invasions from the Continent and border defences were organised to repel Scottish attacks from the North. James had already declared his intention to remain true to the Roman church. He still adhered to the old alliance and had contracted two marriages with the blessing of the French King. However, neither James nor Henry wished to rush into war and both temporised with an agreement to meet at York in September of 1541 to discuss their differences. Henry made the long journey from London but James had been persuaded by this council and clergy that such a meeting was dangerous and he did not attend. When Henry returned to London after this public insult, his anger was exacerbated by the news of the infidelities of Catherine Howard, his fifth Queen. He resolved to make a pre-emptive strike against Scotland.

In August of 1542 English armies crossed the border and burned Roxburgh, Kelso and a number of smaller towns. James mustered the Scottish host but his alienation from the nobility now had its effect. Many lairds from the east coast did not appear and, when the men who had mustered reached Fala Muir near the Lammermuir Hills, they refused to advance into England. In disgust the King returned to Edinburgh and the army disbanded. He was still resolved to attack however and two new armies were raised, one under the Earl of Moray and Cardinal Beaton which would make a diversion in the east and one which would be led by the King himself and would invade from the West. The King's army marched south on the night of the 24th November but James himself was left behind, having fallen ill at Lochmaben. At Solway Moss his army of 10,000 was routed by an English force of only 1,200 men. Although the casualties were relatively few, over a thousand Scots were taken prisoner. The disaster was blamed on a quarrel over who should command the King's army in his absence but the scale of the defeat and the number of prisoners can leave little doubt that the Scots had no heart for the fight.

News was brought to the King as he lay ill at Lochmaben Castle. He returned to Edinburgh and, for a month rode somewhat aimlessly from palace to palace before taking to his bed at Falkland. On the 8th December 1542 the Queen gave birth to her third child, a daughter, Mary. James survived this ultimate blow by less than a week. On receiving news of the birth he is said to have exclaimed, "Adieu, Farewell, it came with a lass, it will pass with a lass". The lack of a male heir seemed certain to give the Kingdom into Henry's hands either, "by his arms or marriage", and there was little hope that the disaffected nobility would rally to the support of an infant girl. Turning his face to the wall James waited for death. On the 14th December, after giving, "a little smile and laughter", to those grouped around his bed, he "held up his hands to God and yielded the spirit". He died a young man, only four months short of his thirty first birthday.

Mary, Queen of Scots
Born 1542
Reigned: 1542-1567
Only surviving legitimate child of James V
Married:
1) Francis, Dauphin of France
2) Lord Darnley
3) James Hepburn, Earl of Bothwell
One son by Darnley
Contemporary of:
Henry VIII 1509-1547
Edward VI 1547-1553
Mary Tudor 1553-1558
Elizabeth I 1558-1603
Beheaded at Fotheringay 1587
Buried at Peterborough and reinterred in Westminster Abbey
in 1612

The death of James V less than a week after the birth of his heir, Mary, plunged Scotland yet again into a long and troubled minority. During these years the country became, more than ever before, a pawn in the struggle between England and Protestantism, and, France and Catholicism. The Auld Alliance was wearing thin with the belief, voiced during the reigns of James IV and James V, that the wars with England were of benefit to none but France. Although this was not the whole truth, Scottish armies had twice refused to cross the border with their king. While the Alliance became less attractive, the Reformation was gathering in strength. James V had remained steadfast in his support of Rome but undercurrents were at work which would ensure that Scotland would be a largely Protestant country before Mary became an adult. It is therefore not surprising that James' death signalled the outbreak of a struggle for power. Nor is it strange that the struggle had both religious and political overtones.

By custom and tradition James Hamilton, the second earl of Arran was the proper Regent for the infant Queen. He was the heir presumptive and, in addition to having leanings towards the reformed faith, he favoured a rapprochement with England. However, Cardinal Beaton, the champion of Roman Catholicism, claimed to have a will written by the late king and naming Beaton as co-Regent to act in concert with the earls of Moray, Huntly and Argyll. Arran countered with the accusation that Beaton had written the will himself and had obtained the king's signature by forcing James to sign blank papers as he lay dying. His charges gained general acceptance. Beaton was arrested and, in the middle of March 1543, parliament declared Arran to be Governor of the Realm.

Henry VIII intervened and took a hand in the affair when he released the Scottish lords captured at Solway Moss and sent them home with bribes given in return for promises that they would aid the English cause. These "assured lords" put their weight behind Arran's natural inclinations and, on July 1, the Scots assented to two treaties. The first was a treaty of marriage between Mary and Henry's son, Prince Edward, to take place when Mary was ten years old; the other, a treaty of peace, was to last until Mary or Edward died.

Had the treaties been fulfilled the sad prophecy of James V, "it (the kingdom) came with a lass, it shall pass with a lass", would have been fulfilled to the letter but, no sooner was agreement reached than Arran, "that most inconstant man in the world", changed his mind. Not only did he change his mind, he changed his religion, re-embraced the Catholic faith and brought Cardinal Beaton and Marie of Guise, both ardent Catholics, into a new council.

Beaton had obtained his liberty in March after only a short term in prison and had shrewdly arranged to bring the fourth earl of Lennox back to Scotland from France. Lennox was important because he was next after Arran in line to the throne and there was some doubt regarding Arran's legitimacy. The earl was the son of his father's second marriage, the first having ended in divorce. If the Catholic church, encouraged by Beaton, were now to declare the divorce, and therefore the second marriage, invalid, Arran would be illegitimate and would lose his place as heir presumptive. He could then no longer claim the position of Regent and the Regency would pass to Lennox, the new heir presumptive. Although there is no proof, it seems likely that Arran was 'reminded' of these possibilities and changed his policy because of the dangers he foresaw to his own position. Reinforcing these private reasons for a change in policy was the general unpopularity of the marriage treaty. Despite the troubles caused by the border wars, and although the Reformation was spreading rapidly, the people had long memories. They, "hated England and stood by France". By December both treaties were annulled, the alliance with France was renewed, the laws against heresy were restored and Beaton was reinstated as chancellor.

Henry VIII reacted to the Scottish change of heart with his, by now, customary belligerence. In 1544 and 1555 he sent troops north to conduct the "rough wooing", a rather ironic description of his use of force in an attempt to persuade the Scots to accept the marriage. Edinburgh, Holyrood and Leith were burned. Seven monasteries were destroyed and there was large scale destruction in Southern Scotland. The only change of heart in Scotland however was that experienced by the "assured lords." Widespread revulsion against the English tactics made them drop their support for the marriage treaty and a form of united government emerged. This was essentially Catholic in nature but Protestant ministers were permitted to preach in Scotland. Beaton, however, had no wish to see the Reformation advance and in the spring of 1546 he arrested and burned George Wishart. The martyrdom led almost directly to Beaton's assassination in the following May. He was killed by a group of Protestants who installed themselves in his castle at St. Andrews and sent an urgent call for help to the English. No assistance was forthcoming and they held out until July 1547 when they surrendered to a French force which attacked in strength. The rebels were imprisoned or, like John Knox, the castle minister, were condemned to penal servitude in the French galleys.

With Henry's death in January 1547, government in England passed to the Protector Somerset who revived the "rough wooing", still in an attempt to force agreement to the marriage of Mary and Edward. In September he won a resounding victory over the Scottish forces at Pinkie near Musselburgh and established a garrison at Haddington only eighteen miles from Edinburgh. The young Queen was sent to Inchmahome Priory on the Lake of Menteith for safety and, in desperation, the Scots appealed for French assistance.

Aid was soon to be forthcoming but conditions were attached. France was eager to keep Scotland as a counterweight to the English and agreed to send troops only if Mary were sent to France and married to the Dauphin. Agreement was reached in July 1548. Action followed swiftly. Mary sailed for France a few weeks later and between 6,000 and 8,000 experienced French troops were sent over to assist in the defence of the realm. Their effect was immediate. Haddington fell and the English were, "clean dung out of Scotland."

The departure of their Queen and the presence of a strong body of French soldiers raised grave problems for the Scots.

The country was free from the fear of immediate English domination but almost everything had been given up to France in exchange. The projected marriage to the Dauphin led the king of France to speak of "one country" and there is little doubt that he looked forward to the day when Scotland would become a dependency of the French crown. It began to look as if Scotland had willingly surrendered to the French what she had fought so long and so hard to protect from the English.

Marie of Guise remained in Scotland after Mary's departure and Arran continued to hold the Regency until 1553 when Mary passed her eleventh birthday. Then it was argued, somewhat dubiously, that, because Mary had now entered her twelfth year, she had reached her majority and was legally entitled to govern in her own name. The normal age of majority was twelve but the argument, put forward by Marie of Guise, was accepted. Under pressure, or with the incentive of bribery, Arran was persuaded to resign and, in the spring of 1554, parliament transferred the government of Scotland to the young Queen's natural choice, her mother.

With Marie of Guise in control, there was an almost immediate increase of French influence, to the extent that the French, "began to think themselves more than masters in Scotland". Little persecution of Protestants was visible however because the problems resulting from Bloody Mary's repressive policy in England were all too apparent. John Knox, having been released from the galleys in 1549, had spent some time in England before wisely retiring to Geneva when Mary Tudor acceded to the throne of England. From there he returned to Scotland for some time during 1555 and was instrumental in forming a Calvinist group among the Scottish nobility. The members of this group became known as the "Lords of the Congregation" and formed the nucleus for the Reformation rebellion. Thus, despite the strong French influence which was reinforced by the attempts of Marie of Guise to preserve Scotland as a Catholic inheritance for her daughter, the Reformation was well under way even before Mary married the Dauphin.

Antipathy towards the French grew stronger as they tightened their hold on the government and in 1577 Knox was invited to return to Scotland to lead a rising which would find men, "ready to jeopard their lives and goods". Second thoughts made the instigators of the plan decide, wisely, that the time was not yet ripe and Knox was hurriedly advised to cancel his journey.

In 1558 Mary Tudor died. Elizabeth was pronounced Queen and, as England reverted to the Protestant faith, Scottish Calvinists began to look south for assistance which might deliver them from the now overwhelming French presence. In the same year Mary married the Dauphin. Both publicly undertook to preserve the laws and customs of Scotland but, in secret, Mary signed documents which would, on her death, give her husband full, and complete, control.

England now had a Protestant Queen who enjoyed the support of the vast majority of her subjects but who, as the daughter of Anne Boleyn, was not recognised by her Catholic subjects because Rome had never recognised the validity of Henry VIII's divorce from his first wife. Scotland, on the other hand, had a Catholic Queen, living and married in France, even though the country was changing rapidly to the reformed faith and was thoroughly disgusted with the pervading French influence. Matters were further complicated however because Mary, descended from Henry VII through the marriage of his daughter Margaret Tudor to James IV, was, in Catholic eyes, the rightful Queen of England. Spain and Rome recognised the realities of the situation and treated Elizabeth as a rightful sovereign but France refused to acknowledge her and viewed the marriage of Mary and the Dauphin as a glorious opportunity to embarrass the English. Politics and religion became inseparable as Mary and her husband assumed the titles, King and Queen of England.

In Scotland the Reformation continued to make gains. Marie of Guise changed her policy of moderation and threatened to repress the Protestants. There was another martyrdom in 1558. Knox sailed from Geneva in May of 1559 and scattered outbreaks of violence occurred in Edinburgh, Linlithgow, Perth and St. Andrews. Government forces were assembled to uphold the law and the Lords of the Congregation reacted by gathering their own army and calling on Elizabeth for assistance. By the end of June the Reformers had occupied Edinburgh and were threatening the nearby port of Leith to which Marie of Guise had withdrawn with the Franch troops. A call for reinforcements was sent to France but assistance was forestalled when English aid for the Reformers arrived in March 1560. It was the first occasion on which English troops were welcomed to Scotland. Still Leith held out but in June Marie of Guise died and the port was starved into surrender. In July the rebellion was finally over and a tripartite agreement was signed by England, France and Scotland. The treaty of Edinburgh recognised Elizabeth's right to the throne of England and ensured the withdrawal of all foreign troops from Scotland. No mention was made of religion but, in August, Parliament met in the name of Mary and her husband Francois. The authority of the Pope was abolished, the celebration of Mass was prohibited and the Calvinist, "Confession of Faith", was adopted as the definition of the official Scottish religion.

In December 1560 Mary's husband died and, with little to look forward to as Queen Dowager of France, she decided to return to Scotland. Elizabeth refused to grant her a safe conduct for the voyage but, although English vessels set out to intercept the convoy, Mary's ships slipped past them in dense fog and landed at Leith in August 1561. It was a grey 'dreich' day. Knox took the weather to be a pattern of things to come and later wrote that the weather reflected the, "sorrow, dolour, darkness and all impiety", that she brought with her. However, despite the apprehension of the Scots Protestants and the polemic of John Knox, Mary made no attempt to change the new Scottish religion and her avowed Catholicism was only indirectly responsible for the troubles she encountered. Certainly there was religious opposition. On the morning after her arrival there was a riot when a private Mass was celebrated in the palace of Holyrood. Throughout her life Mary insisted on her personal right to follow the teachings of the Catholic church but publicly and officially she upheld the Reformed faith. Soon after landing in Scotland she forbade any, "alteration of the state of religion (which) was public and universally standing at her majesty's arrival in this her realm". For some time after the Protestant rebellion the Catholic clergy continued to enjoy the revenues from their lands, but this situation was changed in 1562 when one third of these revenues was collected and shared between the Crown and the Kirk. Knox, who considered that all the revenue from the Catholic benefices should go to the Kirk predictably felt cheated and saw, "two parts freely given to the Devil . . . and the third . . . divided between God and the Devil". Also, in 1562, there were "manifest tokens of disobedience in the North" and Mary permitted Lord James Stewart, a leading Protestant and one of her two advisors, to crush the powerful Catholic earl of Huntly. In the following year leading members of the Catholic clergy were prosecuted for celebrating the Mass in defiance of the proclamation of 1561 which restricted the Mass to the Queen's private chapel alone. Religion, of course, provided a focal point for resentment, particularly for ardent Protestants such as Knox, but Mary's real problems lay in her unresolved dispute with Elizabeth and in her search for, and disastrous choice of, a husband on whom she could rely.

The Treaty of Edinburgh assured Elizabeth of France's recognition of her right to the throne of England but Mary proved a stumbling block when she refused to ratify the treaty. The Queen of Scots considered herself, correctly, as Elizabeth's rightful successor and would not budge from her position until Elizabeth recognised, and proclaimed, her as such. However, Elizabeth was still not sitting too solidly on her own throne and to recognise Mary's right of succession might have provided fuel for the dissatisfied English Catholics. Despite attempts to obtain reciprocal recognition between the two Queens this basic conflict was never resolved until the headsman's axe fell at Fotheringay.

On her return to Scotland Mary was just eighteen years old and her beauty was in full bloom. Tall, athletic and elegant, she was a graceful dancer, an accomplished horsewoman and a most desirable catch in the marriage market of Western Europe. The old earl of Arran, now Duke of Châtelherault, offered his son even before Mary left France. Offers also arrived from the Kings of Sweden and Denmark and from the sons of the Emperor, Charles V. Negotiations were undertaken with Spain on behalf of Don Carlos, son of Philip II but were terminated when Don Carlos became insane in 1564. Despite the problems which such a marriage, into a powerful Catholic family, would raise, the negotiations were supported by Mary's two Protestant advisors, James Stewart and William Maitland. It is unlikely that they expected to bring the discussions to fruition and most probably it was hoped that the possibility of such a match would put pressure on Elizabeth to acknowledge Mary as her successor. To some extent they succeeded. Elizabeth made it quite clear that a marriage with Don Carlos, which would put the might of Spain behind Mary, would create a state of enmity between England and Scotland. It was, however, suggested that marriage to a suitor having Elizabeth's approval would give Mary the recognition she desired. When pressed, Elizabeth named Robert Dudley, her own favourite, as a possible husband for the Scots Queen but such a match was hardly suitable. Nevertheless, the possibility was discussed for several months until Elizabeth announced that any declarations regarding the succession would have to wait until she herself were married or had publicly announced her intention to remain single for the rest of her life. When the negotiations broke down Mary took matters into her own hands and announced her intention of marrying her cousin, Henry Stewart, Lord Darnley. Together, both grandchildren of Henry VII's daughter Margaret Tudor, they linked the strongest claims to the English succession. Darnley had been raised in England and had come to Scotland in 1565. Mary pronounced him, "the lustiest and best proportionit lang man that she had seen", and married him according to Catholic rites on 29 July 1565. The wedding provoked the first serious resistance to the Queen's rule.

James Stewart, earl of Moray and Mary's half brother, had held considerable power as the Queen's chief advisor. He was the eldest surviving bastard son of James V and, had James not remained true to Rome, it is possible that Moray would have succeeded him to the throne. Mary's marriage threatened to nullify all his power. When it became clear that she would brook no interference with her plans he withdrew from the court and conspired with the Duke of Châtelherault whose favoured position as heir presumptive would be lost as soon as an heir was born. When their attempts to arouse resistance to the marriage became obvious Mary issued a proclamation stating that her union with Darnley would in no way affect her established policy towards the Reformed church or to those who preferred the new religion to the old. Nevertheless Moray was able to obtain support from a number of extremist Protestant lords who gathered in force at Stirling. Instead of compromising, Mary ordered Darnley to be given the title, 'King', and immediately married him. Soon after, in August, she raised a Royal army and, with herself at its head, she faced down the Protestant lords, forcing them to flee to England.

Before the end of the year, and indeed within six months of the wedding, Mary had become thoroughly disenchanted with her husband. He showed no kingly qualities and proved to be arrogant, headstrong and intolerant. The Queen refused to give him the 'Crown Matrimonial' which would have enabled him to continue reigning as King if Mary died. Having looked for a man in whom she could place her trust and having chosen badly, Mary now made another serious mistake. Among her courtiers was the foreigner, David Riccio, a musician whom the Queen had grown to trust and who had been advanced to the position of secretary in charge of Mary's French correspondence. Riccio, "that poltroon and vile knave", was rumoured to have great influence and was regarded with deep suspicion. By the protestants he was viewed as a papal agent, by the nobility as a low born upstart who monopolised the Queen's time and company. Dislike and suspicion led to hatred which resulted in a plot to murder Riccio and reinstate Moray and the other lords who had fled to England. Darnley was encouraged to join the conspiracy by his belief, almost certainly unfounded, that Riccio was the Queen's lover. Mary was then six months pregnant. In return for his assistance, the plotters, all Protestant lords, assured him that they would support his desire to have the crown matrimonial. He agreed to help and promised to procure a pardon for Moray when Parliament met on 12 March 1566. Three days before Parliament was due to assemble the conspirators gathered in the Palace of Holyrood while Mary sat in her private room at supper. Riccio and Darnley were both with her when the plotters rushed in, seized Riccio who clung to the Queen's skirts and dragged him screaming into an anteroom where he was stabbed to death. On the following day Sunday 10 March, Darnley cancelled the Parliament which was due to pronounce sentence on Moray and his followers for their earlier rebellion. The next day Moray rode into Holyrood to receive the Royal pardon. Mary was essentially a prisoner in the palace and had no option but to forgive those who had risen in rebellion against her even though, unaware of Moray's complicity, she welcomed him to Edinburgh with the words, "oh my brother, if you had been here, they had not used me thus". However, the Queen was not easily given to submission. Over the weekend she persuaded Darnley to desert the murderers. Early on Tuesday morning they slipped out of the Palace and hurried to the earl of Bothwell's castle at Dunbar where they were joined by the earls of Athol and Huntly and by the lords Seton and Fleming. On the following Sunday, the 17 March, Moray and his adherents fled from the capital and on the following day Mary, in triumph, returned to Edinburgh. The whole affair occupied only ten days.

Riccio's death, and particularly the manner in which it was

accomplished, changed Mary's distaste for Darnley into an active revulsion. Her son, James, was born in the summer of 1566 and by the autumn, with a live healthy heir, she began to look for some means of ridding herself of her husband. Divorce was dangerous because it might cast doubt on the legitimacy of her son, but in November, her councillors, including the earl of Bothwell, assured her that they would find some other means of satisfying her wishes. Mary protested that they must do nothing which would bring her dishonour and was told to, "let us guide the matter among us, and your Grace shall see nothing but good, and approved by Parliament". In December Riccio's murderers received the Queen's pardon and, on their return from exile in England, they were met by Bothwell with a plan to murder Darnley. In January Darnley, who was ill in Glasgow, was brought to Kirk O'Field to convalesce. Mary's apparent reconciliation with him at this time has been put down as a desperate need to rejoin her husband because she had become Bothwell's lover and was carrying his child. She did indeed have a miscarriage in July but explained the twin boys as the result of having been abducted and raped by Bothwell after Darnley's murder. At all events, in the early morning of the 10 February Kirk O'Field was "blown up wi powder". Darnley was discovered dead in the garden still in his nightgown. No solid evidence exists whereby guilt can be unequivocally established but the citizens of Edinburgh had no doubt that responsibility for the murder lay directly with Bothwell. Pressure rose for the murderers to be brought to justice and on 12 April, Bothwell was tried before Parliament in a private action raised by the earl of Lennox, father of the late king. After seven hours Bothwell was, "made clean of the slaughter albeit that it was heavily murmured that he was guilty thereof". Although the legal formalities were strictly observed the verdict was largely due to the absence of Lennox, the accuser. Bothwell's followers, said to number four thousand, swarmed the streets of Edinburgh making it impossible for Lennox to attend.

Mary now made her third disastrous mistake. Within a

month of Bothwell's acquittal she married him in a Protestant ceremony despite many warnings to the contrary. Whether Mary entered the marriage willingly or not is unclear. Less than a week after the trial she had gone to Stirling to visit her son. On her return to Edinburgh she was intercepted by Bothwell and taken to Dunbar. Later she claimed to have been forcibly abducted and raped. Her marriage, she said, had been undertaken only to preserve her honour. However, friends and enemies alike both agreed that she had become overly familiar with Bothwell since Riccio's murder. Few people believed her tale of abduction and rape. Marriage to the man popularly believed to have killed her husband convinced many that the Queen herself had been a party to the killing.

With her wedding on May 15 Mary lost the support of virtually all the nobility and most of the population. Bothwell had no great power base but he had powerful enemies and an army was raised with the intention of setting the Queen 'free', ensuring the safety of Prince James and bringing the murderers to impartial justice. Exactly a month after the wedding Mary and Bothwell faced their enemies near Musselburgh. The Queen's army dwindled because of desertions and, after ensuring that Bothwell made his escape, Mary surrendered. She was led back to Edinburgh through crowds shouting, "Burn the whore", to be imprisoned in the island castle at Lochleven. Bothwell fled from Scotland and eventually reached Denmark where he was imprisoned and where he died. Mary never saw her third husband again.

At Lochleven Mary was compelled to abdicate in favour of her son who was proclaimed King James VI. At the end of July 1567 she miscarried and became very sick, but, despite her illness during this period, she did not give up hope of regaining the crown. On 2 May 1568 the Queen escaped and revoked her abdication. Nine earls, eighteen lords and nine bishops rallied to her cause and within a short time she had raised an army of between five and six thousand men, almost twice the size of the army of the Regent Moray, her half brother. With a desire to avoid relying too heavily on any one of her followers it was decided to march towards the relatively neutral ground of Dumbarton where her strength might be built up even further. Numerical superiority caused her army to bypass Glasgow rather closer than was altogether wise. Moray was established near the small village of Langside. As the vanguard of Mary's troops came within sight of the Regent's position they immediately attacked but the main body of her troops failed to follow up the charge. It was afterwards explained that, Argyll, the leader of the Marian army, had either fainted or suffered from an epileptic fit at the crisis of the battle. His leaderless troops fell away in confusion and the result was a resounding success for the Regent. Mary watched the battle from the top of a nearby hill. When it became clear that her army was routed she slipped away to the South. Three days later, in a small fishing boat, she crossed the Solway Firth into England.

The decision to choose England over France was made by Mary alone. Elizabeth had shown sympathy during her imprisonment at Lochleven and Mary obviously hoped for assistance. But sympathy at long range was very different from any desire to restore Mary to the throne. Her presence was a source of considerable embarrassment to Elizabeth. Any fellow monarch cast out by rebellious subjects compelled concern but Mary was the Queen who had claimed to be the rightful Queen of England. Indeed she was still recognised as such by many Catholics in England and on the Continent. Elizabeth could take no action against her. She could not do anything which might be construed as giving aid to the rebels but neither could she offer assistance which might make her own seat on the throne of England less secure. Initially she temporised. The Queen of Scots was received as a guest and, at Mary's request, Elizabeth initiated an enquiry into the rebellion. Moray came south to defend the rebel cause, claiming that Mary was unfit to govern because of her recent behaviour over Darnley and Bothwell. The casket letters, Mary's correspondence with Bothwell, were produced. They proved to be so damaging to the

Queen's reputation that her honour was torn in shreds and her hopes were lost. The original letters have since disappeared and it is now impossible to say whether or not they were forgeries as has so often been claimed. In January 1569 the inquiry was completed with a suitably ambivalent decision. Regarding the rebel lords Elizabeth proclaimed that, "there has been nothing deduced against them as yet that may impair their honour and allegiances". In almost the same breath she declared that the nobles had produced no evidence, "whereby the Queen of England should conceive or take any evil opinion of the Queen, her good sister, for anything yet seen". With neither party declared guilty, the status quo was preserved. Moray returned to Scotland to continue as Regent. Mary remained in England.

Still Mary did not relinquish her hope of being re-established on the throne of Scotland. Although she was now virtually a prisoner, many Scots remained loyal and opposed the rule of Moray. Gradually, however, their influence was reduced until, in the early 1570's, Edinburgh Castle alone stood out against, "the King's men". By this time Mary had begun to look to the English Catholics and to Spain for her release. She was implicated in a Catholic plot in 1572. Elizabeth, realising the need to preserve a friendly, Protestant, Scotland, finally acted. In May of the following year English troops marched north to assist in bringing about the submission of Edinburgh Castle. Increasingly Mary became the focus of Catholic plots designed to restore the Roman faith in England. In 1585 she was involved in the conspiracy planned by Anthony Babington. Correspondence was discovered in which Mary had apparently agreed to the assassination of Elizabeth. The letters proved to be fatal. At long last, with no real enthusiasm for the deed, and under heavy pressure from her councillors, Elizabeth signed the death warrant. Before she could change her mind it was sent to Fotheringay and, on 8 February 1587, Mary was led to the block declaring, "I am settled in the ancient Roman Catholic religion and mind to spend my blood in defence of it". Buried at Peterborough, her body was reinterred at

Westminster in 1612. Today she lies close to Elizabeth in the sanctuary of Westminster Abbey.

Of all their monarchs the Scots remember Mary with deep affection. Her tomb is rarely without a small sprig of heather lovingly placed by some admirer born nearly 400 years after her death.

James VI

Born 1566
Reigned: 1567-1625 (King of England 1603-1625)
Only son of Mary, Queen of Scots, and Lord Darnley
Married Anne, daughter of Frederick II of Denmark and
Norway
Seven children
Contemporary of: Elizabeth I 1558-1603
Died at his favourite residence, Theobalds, near London
Buried at Westminster

On July 29, 1567, at the tender age of thirteen months, James VI was crowned by the Protestant Bishop, Adam Bothwell who anointed him, "on ye croune of the head, shoulder blaides, palmes of ye hands, saiing certain prayers before in the English tongue". Knox preached a sermon, the Queen's abdication was proclaimed, and the event was celebrated with "fyre works, shotting of cannon and feasting".

For most of his youth the king lived in Stirling castle under the care of the Earl and Countess of Mar. Soon after his third birthday he was considered ready to begin the long process of learning the necessary accomplishments of a monarch. Two tutors were appointed, George Buchanan and Peter Young. Buchanan was an elderly gentleman over sixty years old and was the leading Scottish scholar of the day. He had studied in Paris and St. Andrews and had spent a considerable part of his life overseas before returning to Scotland in 1561. Although initially acceptable to Mary because of his international outlook they became estranged after Mary married Darnley. Later he became one of the Queen's principal detractors, writing pamphlets for the "king's party" and helping to prepare accusations against Mary when she was deposed. Buchanan was a rather fierce old man and, under his instruction, James absorbed a deep and thorough classical education. He became a capable linguist. He grew to love books, and his native intelligence, combined with the education he received at the hands of his tutors, made him one of the, "most learned of sovereigns". Buchanan's task was not, however, restricted to providing a formal education. He also instilled the Protestant faith and Calvinist theology in his young charge and attempted to develop in him the attitude of a constitutional monarch. James was taught that his mother had been a whore, that the church and state were separate but equal, and that rebellion was justified against tyrannical rulers. Although most of Buchanan's teachings were readily absorbed, the king resisted his political theories. The idea of a monarch circumscribed by a powerful church became abhorrent as James grew older. In direct contrast to the indoctrination attempted by Buchanan, he leaned towards an episcopal system in which the crown would control the church through Bishops appointed by, and responsible to, the king. Later he carried his beliefs to their logical conclusion and formulated his theory of the special relationship between God, the King and his people — The Divine Right of Kings.

Buchanan was not a kindly man. He browbeat the young king to such an extent that, in later years, James found himself trembling at the very sight of courtiers who "reminded him of his pedagogue". The relationship with his other tutor was quite different. Peter Young was only twenty-seven years old when appointed to his position in the Royal household. Although most of the responsibility for James' education lay with Buchanan, Young encouraged his studies and acted like a youthful uncle. His kindness was rewarded with the King's affection and trust.

Until a few months before the Monarch's twelfth birthday Scotland was ruled by a series of Regents. When she was compelled to abdicate Mary had been forced to recognise the Regency of her half brother, the Earl of Moray. At that time neither Moray nor the infant king commanded much support in the country. Antagonism towards Mary had largely evaporated and had been replaced with sympathy for her plight. Most of the common people, and many of the nobility, had little love for the new order and Mary's escape from Lochleven castle could have precipitated a crisis had her army not been defeated at Langside. The flight to England and her subsequent detention there gave Moray the opportunity to win Scotland over to the King's party. He proved to be a good and capable ruler. Wise and just policies commanded respect, but, although support for the Regency increased as time passed, the Marian party still held important castles at Doune, Dumbarton and Edinburgh by the time of Moray's death in 1570. His murder resulted from a feud of the type which had become common during Scottish minorities.

In the previous minority, that of Queen Mary, the country had been ruled by James Hamilton, earl of Arran and later Duke of Châtelherault. His influence waned as Mary's mother, Marie of Guise, obtained a more dominating role and in 1554 his regency had been terminated. When Mary returned to Scotland to rule in her own right Châtelherault had proposed his son as a husband for the Young Queen but the offer was spurned. Later, after Mary married Darnley, the Duke took part in the abortive rebellion organised largely by Moray but was pardoned on condition that he lived in exile for at least five years. Returning to Scotland in 1569 he opposed Moray's Regency and became the nominal head of the Queen's party. He himself was relatively inactive but others of the Hamilton family were less prepared to stand by and watch their power disappear entirely. On January 30 1570, James Hamilton of Bothwellhaugh shot Moray as he rode through the town of Linlithgow. The house from which the shot was fired was owned by Archbishop Hamilton, Châtelherault's half brother, and another Hamilton, Châtelherault's son, provided a horse for the assassin's escape. Moray's death could have had serious effects on the fortunes of the King's party but a raid on the border by those who still supported Mary provided the necessary justification for an attack on the Hamiltons who were held responsible. A small English force came north to seek reprisals. Joined by soldiers of the King's party they ravaged the Hamilton lands and destroyed the palace, castle and town of Hamilton.

Moray was replaced by the Earl of Lennox, father of the unfortunate Darnley. The earl commanded little respect among the nobility but he enjoyed the support of Elizabeth and was the natural choice as the young king's grandfather. He ruled for just over a year during which the Earl of Morton rose to become the effective leader of the king's party. Together they subdued the castles of Doune and Dumbarton and brought Archbishop Hamilton to the scaffold. Then, turning their attention to Edinburgh castle, which still held out for Mary, Morton organised a siege from the nearby port of Leith. The city became largely deserted in the summer of 1571 due to the possibility of military action, and Morton himself left in August to attend Parliament in Stirling. His departure from command of the siege and the gathering of their leading opponents at Stirling encouraged the defenders of the castle to strike a blow for Mary. As the last Marian stronghold in Scotland the castle had become isolated and desperate measures seemed necessary. A night attack was planned with the primary objective of taking prisoners so that negotiations could be conducted from a position of strength. The raid was timed to occur when Parliament was about to disperse. Initially successful it was foiled only because the attackers failed to withdraw with their hostages as quickly as had been planned. The delay provided time for news to be sent to the castle. Mar quickly gathered a small force and rode into town to intercept them. Most of the prisoners they had taken were freed in the subsequent fight, but the Regent, Lennox, was shot in the back and was carried back to the castle mortally wounded. Parliament hastily reassembled and elected the earl of Mar to succeed him. Within a year he also had died. Some said his death occurred because, "he loved peace and could not have it", but rumours suggested that he had been poisoned by the Lord of Morton who had entertained him shortly before he fell ill. "Some of his friends and the vulgar suspected that he had gotton wrong at his banquet". Nevertheless, in 1572, the Regency was transferred to Morton who held the office for the next six years.

Despite the rumours which circulated after Mar's death, the new Regent was the logical choice. He had become the effective leader of the King's party after Moray was shot in 1570 and would have been chosen as Regent as far back as 1567 had Moray declined to accept the offer. He had been Chancellor during the brief period of Mary's reign and had held office until dismissed for his complicity in the murder of Riccio. Thereafter he had firmly opposed the Queen. On his return to Scotland in 1566, when Riccio's murderers were pardoned, he had been approached by Bothwell with an invitation to join the plot against Darnley but, as far as is known, he took no direct part in the murder. After Mary's enforced abdication it was Morton who 'discovered' the Casket letters which would ensure the Queen's detention in England, her honour tarnished and her reputation in shreds.

Morton was installed on November 24 1572. The most pressing problem continued to be the resistance of the Marian party in Edinburgh castle. The only assistance they could expect locally would come from the Hamiltons and Morton neutralised that source of possible support as soon as possible. In 1573 he and the Hamiltons came to terms and signed the "Pacification of Perth" which offered a general pardon to all who had fought on Mary's side in the recent civil war. Then he turned his attention to the castle and approached Elizabeth I for assistance in obtaining its surrender. The Queen of England had taken a relatively inactive part in the struggle which was waged in Scotland after Mary fled from Langside but, by 1573, Mary had become fairly heavily involved in Catholic plots, in particular, the Ridolfi plot of the previous year. Elizabeth, now excommunicated, realised that a friendly, Protestant, Scotland was essential to maintain stability. In May English artillery was sent north to pound down the walls. The castle fell on 29th and Mary's last remaining power base was gone.

During the next five years Scotland was kept, "under great obedience". Supported by Elizabeth, Morton pursued a policy of friendship with England. Unlike many of those who had held the Regency in previous minorities he felt responsible for preserving the kingdom in good order for the benefit of the people and the king and wrote that, when James felt ready to assume, "his own government . . . none shall more willingly agree and advance the same nor I, since I think never to set my face against him whose honour, safety and preservation have been so dear to me". But Morton had enemies and was disliked by the members of the king's household. To the young James he seemed an austere man, more concerned with affairs of state than with the feelings, or wishes, of the king. Gradually, as the enmity towards Morton filtered through the members of James' entourage, the king himself developed a strong aversion towards him. When an opportunity came to dispose of his services, James took it without regret.

Morton's troubles rose out of a private feud between the earls of Argyll and Athol. When summond to defend themselves against lawful punishment they buried their quarrel and saw an opportunity to use James' dislike of the Regent to destroy his power. Instead of submitting to Morton, Argyll approached the king directly and asked him to summon the nobility to Stirling where he and Athol would present their disagreement and accept the judgement, not of Morton, but of the King and the nobles. James agreed, but such an abrogation of his powers as Regent was too much for Morton to bear. He approached James to protest against the method chosen to resolve the quarrel and offered his resignation in the event that James could not alter his plans. As so often happens in such cases the resignation was accepted. The King's "acceptance of the government" was proclaimed in March of 1578 even though he was still short of his twelfth birthday. Despite his former protestations, Morton saw clearly that such a young Monarch could be easily manipulated. Without hesitation he acted to preserve his authority and quickly gained control of Stirling castle and the person of the King. Athol and Argyll raised an army against him and the nation might have been plunged into civil war had not the English Ambassador offered to mediate. His efforts were rewarded with a compromise instead of battle. Morton did not regain the Regency but remained as First Lord of the Council with the King in nominal command. When Athol died in 1579 Morton was again suspected of having used poison but the rumours did him no harm and he soon achieved a position of pre-eminence. He now took action against the Hamiltons who had been involved in the death of Moray. By the end of the summer most of the Hamilton family had been banished from the court. The sons of the late Duke of Châtelherault were forced to flee from the country and a number of Hamilton castles were destroyed. Again it appeared that Morton was in full control.

In September of 1579 the King's cousin, Esmé Stewart, arrived in Scotland. He was the grandson of the third earl of Lennox and had advanced close to the throne in the line of succession because of the death of Darnley's brother and the forfeiture of the Hamiltons. About twenty four years older than the King himself, Esmé was handsome and likeable. James had few close relations. He welcomed his cousin warmly and showered him with honours. In 1580 Stewart was created earl of Lennox and in the following year was raised to the Dukedom. He was given command of the King's bodyguard and, in view of his meteoric rise, it is not surprising that he developed ambitions to replace Morton. But Morton was still very powerful and could not be attacked directly. Instead, Lennox arranged for a well born soldier, Captain James Stewart, to accuse the 'First Lord' of having been involved in the murder of Darnley. Although Morton swore an oath that he had not been involved in the crime he did admit that he had not warned Darnley of the plot although he had known of its existence. This was sufficient to ensure his condemnation. At the beginning of

June 1581 he was publicly executed in Edinburgh. For his reward James Stewart, who was surprisingly enough the brother-in-law of John Knox, was created earl of Arran. Lennox became essentially a "pseudo Regent" and enjoyed complete authority. But Esmé Stewart, now Duke of Lennox, was hardly acceptable in such an exalted position. Although outwardly converted to the Reformed faith he had been a Roman Catholic prior to his arrival in Scotland. Rumours of Catholic plots to restore Queen Mary still circulated and although there was little or no tangible evidence, the ministers of the kirk strongly suspected that Lennox was, in reality, a Papal agent. Even Elizabeth was concerned at the turn of events and sent warning letters to the King. In January of 1581 Lennox and James attempted to fend off the criticism by publishing the, "Negative Confession", which denied all doctrine not acceptable to the kirk. In March the 'Confession' was ordered to be proclaimed throughout the country but, despite their efforts, it did little to stifle opposition. The nobility were also concerned because of the sudden rise to power of Lennox and Arran. In August 1582 they acted. Invited to take part in a hunting party by William Ruthven, first earl of Gowrie, the king was seized at Perth and forced to accompany his abductors to Ruthven castle. The, "Ruthven raiders", held James until July 1583. Shortly after they had obtained possession of his person, Lennox was compelled to leave Scotland and Arran was disgraced. But James escaped after about ten months in captivity and Gowrie had little opportunity to enjoy the rewards of his raid. Arran was restored to favour, Gowrie was executed and most of the others involved fled to England. With them went a number of leading ministers including John Knox and Andrew Melville, the leader of the Presbyterian party.

Melville's flight was necessary because, in October 1582, six months before the king escaped, the General Assembly of the kirk had formally approved of the Ruthven raid. The ministers, with their deep rooted suspicions of Lennox, regarded James' capture as having saved, "the true religion

. . . from evident and certain dangers". The "dangers" certainly related to the rapid rise of Lennox and the rumours that he was a Papal agent but underlying the whole affair was the friction caused by the kirk's struggle to break free from the Crown. Melville saw the church and state as two quite separate kingdoms and clearly believed in the superiority of the kingdom of God, a kingdom in which James was, "not a king, nor a lord, nor a head, but a member". At a very early age James had met the same sort of ideas from his tutor, Buchanan. He had not accepted them then and did not do so now. As he grew older, the king found himself totally opposed to Melville's conception of the presbyterian relationship among God, the King and the people. He considered the presbyterian model to agree, "as well with monarchy as God and the Devil", and believed it impossible for any monarch to govern effectively with a powerful and independent church looking over his shoulder and criticising every move. The solution, for James, was a reformed church organised along episcopal lines with Bishops chosen by, and responsible to, the Crown. "No Bishops, no King", became his watch word, an attitude to which Melville and the kirk were utterly opposed.

The events which followed the King's escape from Ruthven Castle appeared to move Scotland far along the path to Episcopacy. The earl of Arran regained his former power but to a much greater extent because Lennox had died in exile. With James now thoroughly annoyed at the Kirk's approval of his abduction the, "Black Acts", were passed in May 1584. These affirmed the King's authority over the church in spiritual matters, made decisions by the church invalid unless approved by the king, prohibited sermons criticising the king and decreed that the church would be governed by Bishops appointed by the King. Although this represented a negation of almost all Knox and Melville had worked for, the effect was short lived. In England, Gowrie's former allies plotted another attempt to remove Arran. With some assistance from Elizabeth, who did not fully appreciate the dangers of Presbyterianism, they returned to Scotland in the Autumn of 1585. For a time it looked as if there might be civil war but Arran failed to respond to the challenge of the "Protestant lords", and fell from power as a result. Andrew Melville now also returned and a compromise between church and state was worked out. Bishops would no longer be chosen directly by the king. Although James would still initiate the choice, their appointment would depend on obtaining the approval of the General Assembly. Equally important they would not be responsible to the king but to a series of local presbyteries.

Throughout his youth James had been educated to think of himself as the true heir to the throne of England and he was in a most difficult and sensitive position when his mother became implicated in the Babington plot against Elizabeth in 1586. Scotland and England had just concluded a formal alliance in which Elizabeth had promised not to take any action which would deprive James of "his rights" respecting the succession, even though she would not officially acknowledge him as her successor. He had no love or affection for his mother, having been separated from her as a baby. He had been taught that Mary's reign had been disastrous for his country, that she herself had been bereft of honour and that she had married his father's murderer by whom she was already pregnant when the murder occurred. Mary's continued presence in England had always constituted a threat to his throne because the great Catholic powers persisted in their hopes to bring about a revival of the Roman faith with her restoration. Yet, despite these compelling reasons to see her impending death as having only advantages for him, she was his mother and James could not view the possibility of her execution without unease. When she was found guilty of conspiring to procure the death of Elizabeth he sent two ambassadors to protest against the death sentence. Their efforts may well have been no more than an empty gesture because he must have known that their arguments would carry little weight in England and no other significant actions were taken to delay the due process of the law. On 1 February 1587 the death warrant was signed. Mary was executed on the 8th. There was talk of revenge in Scotland but the King would have none of it. Whatever fleeting doubts he had about the correct course to follow he clearly saw his future as the next King of England and could hardly have expected to indulge in reprisals over a mother he could not remember, for whom he had no affection and whose death enhanced the security of his crown.

The approach of the Spanish Armada in the following year showed the first significant example of James', "Kingcraft". Throughout his life he studiously avoided the blatant use of force to impose solutions to the problems which vexed him, preferring to steer a middle course, to be "all things to all men" and to use political skill, his, "Kingcraft", to bring about the desired result. Inevitably, while working quietly to achieve his own aims, it became necessary to plan, and insure, for the possibility that these desires might not be realised in the immediate future or in the manner in which he had planned. The express purpose of the Armada was to topple Elizabeth and restore Catholicism in England. Hoping that it would not succeed and so upset his plans for the succession, James prepared the Scottish defences. However, in the event that England was defeated there was a distinct possibility that he would be confirmed as King of Scotland and England provided he converted to the Roman faith. For this to happen he would need the support of the Scottish Catholics and he therefore did nothing to inhibit the intrigues of the Catholic Earls who were scheming in favour of Spain. With the defeat of the Armada and the destruction of the survivors in the awful storm which blew their galleons round the northern tip of Scotland, the prospect of Catholicism receded. Still however, there were plots afoot in the North where the majority of the people were still inclined to favour Rome. In February of 1589 letters from the Catholic Earls to the King of Spain were intercepted by English agents. Huntly and two other Earls had written to express regret at the failure of the Armada and to suggest that any future invasion should be launched by Spanish troops landed in Scotland. Elizabeth forwarded the letters to James with an urgent request to have the correspondents imprisoned. But James realised no doubt that their plans had been directed against Elizabeth rather than himself. Although Huntly was confined to Edinburgh Castle he was released after a few days. In this, and other, intrigues James showed great leniency, or perhaps a desire to keep a foot in both camps. Certainly many people suspected his motives but it is unlikely that he had any serious thoughts of converting to the Roman faith after the Armada failed. His lack of severity in dealing with the Catholic Earls was most likely prompted by other reasons. There is no doubt that he preferred political manoeuvering to the application of brute force. He himself had a poor physique and was no lover of the martial arts although he was a good, tireless, horseman. His personal courage has been called into question and used to explain his forgiving attitude but it is more probable that his treatment of the powerful catholic families was governed by a keen understanding of the kinship network which riddled sixteenth century Scotland. Severe action against powerful malcontents might well have given rise, as in the not too distant past, to blood feuds and enmities which would be passed down from father to son. The king preferred to deal with affairs in other, more subtle, ways. Even so he was not averse to the use of force when necessary. After Huntly's release the earl was involved in a conspiracy to move armies on Edinburgh simultaneously from the North and from the border country. James did not hesitate to respond to this challenge. Loyal lords were summoned to defend the capital and the threat on Edinburgh disappeared. He quickly moved his troops north following the retreating army led by Huntly, Bothwell and Errol and accepted their chastened surrender at the Brig O' Dee. The traitors were imprisoned as before but, once again, were released and restored to favour. In 1592 Huntly was involved in the murder of, "The Bonnie Earl of Moray", and, no sooner had the outcry against him died down, than he was discovered to be again entangled in a conspiracy with Spain. At the end of the year letters were discovered mentioning plans to bring Spaniards into Scotland, to overthrow the monarchy and to restore the Roman faith. With the correspondence were blank documents which were to be sent to Spain to receive details of the invasion plans. The "Spanish blanks" were signed by Huntly, Errol and Angus. James marched north in force to deal with them but, when Huntly and his allies withdrew to the North West, the King did not follow them. Once again he showed surprising leniency. The traitors were not forfeited in the Parliament which met in July 1593 and, when Huntly and Errol finally submitted in October, James decided that no action would be taken against them provided they renounced Catholicism or went into voluntary exile. Both were forfeited when they refused the King's offer but the penalty had little effect in dampening their religious ardour. In July of the following year a known Papal agent and three strangers, "suspected to be Papists", were arrested when they disembarked from a ship at Aberdeen. It was impossible to hold them for trial however, because Huntly, Angus and Errol immediately arrived with a large body of supporters, threatened to invade the city with "fyre and sword" and carried the prisoner off to safety. By the time of their raid on Aberdeen, they had been joined by the Earl of Bothwell, a Protestant, who had previously carried out a lone reign of terrorism and who was probably insane. He had been arrested in 1591 for having employed witchcraft against the king and had later been outlawed after his escape from prison. From then until 1593 he followed an erratic course of single handed attacks on Royal Palaces apparently in a rather misguided effort to restore his good favour in the eyes of the king. In spite of, or perhaps because of, his methods of achieving this aim he enjoyed the support of some of the most extreme members of the kirk who saw him as a, "sanctified scourge", who might, by his terrorism, force James away from his now highly suspicious policy of leniency towards the Catholic Earls. In July of 1593 Bothwell forced his way into the king's bedchamber at Holyrood with a naked sword which he symbolically laid at James' feet in a last attempt to show his loyalty and thus regain his forfeited lands. The show of bare steel did not, however, dispose the king favourably towards him and, after one further unsuccessful attack in the Spring of 1594, he fled north to seek refuge with his kinsman, Huntly.

With Huntly and Bothwell now acting together, the king and the kirk joined forces although their temporary unification was effected with quite different purposes in mind. James wished to hunt out and destroy Bothwell whom he saw as the greater damage because of his personal attacks. The kirk, on the other hand, had become greatly concerned about the effect which the Catholic Earls might have if their freedom to intrigue were not curtailed. In the autumn of 1594 a Royal army, accompanied by the kirk in the person of Andrew Melville, marched into Aberdeenshire against the rebels. Huntly and Errol surrendered, their houses were destroyed and they were forced into exile. Bothwell escaped and wandered abroad until he died in 1624 but, within two years the Catholic Earls were back in Scotland and were again received warmly into the Royal favour. In the long run, James' 'kingcraft' had paid off. After their return the northern earls took no further part in Catholic intrigues. By combining leniency together with the show of force when necessary James had resolved a conflict which in previous centuries would almost certainly have resulted in a prolonged and bloody civil war.

James' bloodless solution to the difficulties raised by the Catholic Earls ensured their eventual compliance with the royal authority but raised problems in other areas. His leniency was inextricably bound up with conflict between church and crown because, to the ministers, it seemed that he was quite unwilling to repress Papacy with the thoroughness they would have wished. Unwittingly the northern earls provided the spur with which the Presbyterian system was advanced. The effect of the "Black Acts" of 1584 had been alleviated two years later when the Protestant lords returned from England and ousted the earl of Arran who had been raised to power by the suspected Papal agent Esmé Stewart, Earl of Lennox. In 1587 the Presbyterian cause had, again unwittingly, been further advanced by the "Act of Annexation" whereby lands formerly granted to the church were annexed by the crown. James' sole intention was to relieve his pressing financial problems but he quite failed to foresee that the removal of rich lands from the church would have other, far reaching, effects. By removing from the church a source of revenue which would have been enjoyed by its highest dignitaries, the King's Bishops, he removed much of the incentive for his own men to serve him in that capacity. Then, following the murder of the Bonnie Earl of Moray, the public outcry was so great that James was constrained to yield even more. He passed the "Golden Act" in which the Presbyterian organisation of the church was accepted and the "Black Acts" were, to a large extent, repudiated.

When Huntly returned from exile to be received warmly by the king there was another outbreak of hostility. This time however matters went too far and James was able to recoup much of his ground. After repeated criticism from the General Assembly and individual ministers in 1596, there was a riot in Edinburgh which gave the king the opportunity to leave the city, denounce the ministers and the burgesses and to declare that Edinburgh would no longer be the capital. Within a short time the city regained its status but only after a large fine had been imposed and the king had insisted that the future appointment of ministers in the larger cities must meet with his approval. He now went on the offensive. The support of much of the nobility was obtained by awarding grants, or bribes, from the annexed lands and James clearly used part of the "Golden Act" to gain an overall ascendancy. The extremist ministers who strongly opposed James' claim to authority over the church were distributed fairly thinly in the country. Most resided in the large cities in the south. Although the "Golden Act" had given the kirk the right to call General Assemblies, the king was left with the authority, at each Assembly, to name the date and place of the next. Accordingly James ensured that meetings of the Assembly took place in areas where he could be assured of support, or at least more support than he would get in Edinburgh.

Gradually an Episcopal system was imposed. The General Assembly of 1597 appointed Commissioners, "to give advice to his majesty in all affairs concerning the welfare of the church". Careful handling of the situation ensured that he was only given the advice he wanted. In 1600 representatives of the kirk, selected by the king from a list drawn up by the kirk, were admitted to Parliament. This might have been thought a big step forward for the Presbyterians but, traditionally, only Bishops had represented the Church in Parliament. The Assembly was very careful to note that its representatives were 'Commissioners' not Bishops, but the first steps had been taken. Within ten years, after James had assumed the crown of England, the kirk had been sufficiently tamed to accept Bishops with all that they entailed.

For much of the duration of his rule as King of Scots, James was under the influence of others and it has proved difficult to determine the point at which he began to shape his own policies. When he did so, it became obvious that he preferred diplomacy to force and was determined to do away with the blood feuds which were endemic to earlier ages. In 1587, when he was still only eleven years old, he earnestly urged the nobles attending a banquet at Holyrood to be friends with one another. On the morning after the feast he marched them through Edinburgh forcing bitter enemies to hold hands and walk side by side to the market cross where they were presented with wine and made to toast each other, swearing oaths to peace and friendship. The performance was repeated again eight years later in an effort to solve arguments which had led to feuds and, although it took a long time, James eventually persuaded even the more turbulent of his nobles to resort to the law instead of reaching for their swords. During the 1590's he was largely independent of external personal influences and, after the power of the extremist Catholics and Protestants was broken in 1597, he began to emerge as the most effective king the country had ever seen. During his last years in Scotland there was a significant decrease in violence and a contrasting increase in respect for law and order, broken only by the

Gowrie conspiracy of 1600 when the two sons of the executed earl of Gowrie were killed during an apparent attempt to kidnap the king.

In the Highlands he tried new means of control and preferred not to use the traditional methods which had relied largely upon one family or clan, the king's agents, to police the area. Instead he sought to make the chiefs responsible for the behaviour of their people and forced them to find lowlanders of means to stand surety for their own good behaviour. There was an attempt to colonise the outer Isles by "Gentlemen Adventurers of Fife in 1599". They were given large areas of forfeited land in the expectation that it would prove fertile and would respond to good husbandry. The land was to be held free of crown rent for seven years but the Islemen were antagonistic, supplies were insufficient and many of the 'colonists' succumbed to illness. After three attempts the project was abandoned.

From about 1596, James' primary interest was focussed on his desire to follow Elizabeth on the throne of England. As the century ran to its conclusion it became obvious that her reign could not last much longer and Cecil, the most powerful man in England, began to cultivate the King of Scots as her most likely successor. Scotland as a whole was united in its wish to see their king obtain the glory inherent in Elizabeth's crown. English Protestants favoured him and English Catholics, because of his dealings with the Catholic Earls of Scotland, were not afraid of repression or persecution. When Elizabeth died on 24 March 1603 there was no hesitation to declare that "James, King of Scotland was, now become our only lawful, lineal and rightful lord, James the First King of England". The news was brought to Holyrood only three days after Elizabeth died. Assuring his Scottish subjects that he would visit them, "every three years or oftener as I shall have occasion", James departed on April 5. He returned only once, in 1617, but governed Scotland at long range to such good effect that, during the reign of his son, Charles I, the Scots looked back with regret to, "the wisdom of the blessed king James".

Postscript

Postscript

The union of the crowns in 1603 was effected smoothly and had little immediate effect north of the border. Scotland was well governed by able administrators. The law was strongly enforced and the Highlands and the Isles at last became fully integrated parts of the Kingdom.

The union of the Parliaménts, a century later, was altogether another matter. At the beginning of the eighteenth century, Scotland was in the throes of a severe economic depression. The Darien scheme of 1688 and 1689 had failed disastrously. Trade had fallen off, unemployment was rife and many considered that the problems had been brought about by unwarranted English interference in Scottish affairs or, more particularly, "through the removal of our kings into another country". The suppression of the Conventicles and the "killing times" of the 1670's were not long past and, whereas one part of the country remembered these with bitterness, another part was beginning to organise ways and means of restoring the 'rightful' Stuart line.

When the crown passed to Queen Anne, daughter of James VII (and II), it began to look as if Scotland might break away to reassert her former independence as a sovereign state. Being without a direct heir, the death of Anne would have raised problems of succession and the English Parliament had passed an act decreeing that, on Anne's death, the English crown would pass to the House of Hanover. No such act was passed in Scotland, however, and in 1702 Queen Anne's Parliament made its first serious approach to the Scots with a view to obtaining Union. Scotland's Commissioners rejected their proposal, largely because the English were still not prepared to allow the Scots access to their profitable overseas trade. Discontent smouldered on both sides of the border. The English were annoyed by the intransigence of the Scots, and the Scots began to fear the imposition on Scotland of a king chosen by the English. Scottish tempers rose. An English ship, thought to have been involved in the sinking of one of the Darien expedition vessels, was impounded at Leith and some of the crew were hanged. Militia were raised, gunpowder was imported, and preparations were made for the war which appeared more and more likely. In 1706 new proposals, of much greater benefit to Scotland, were made and, after a number of secret meetings between English and Scots Commissioners, these were accepted.

Publication of the proposals for Union roused fierce opposition. Riots broke out in Glasgow and Edinburgh and there was a short lived rising of Covenantors. Petitions, protests and pamphlets decrying the union were circulated, but to no avail. On 16 January 1707 the Act of Union passed through the final stages.

The process of unification began in earnest in 1503 when James IV married the sister of Henry VIII, Margaret Tudor, as part of a general settlement with England. The marriage did not go unopposed. Although Scotland was mainly in favour the English Privy Council objected that the joining of the two Royal families might well lead to a Scots king sitting on the English throne. Henry VII, Margaret's father, took a more longterm view. "Supposing", he said, "which God forbid, that all my male progeny should become extinct, and the kingdom devolve by law to Margaret's heirs, will England be damaged thereby? For since it ever happens that the less becomes subservient to the greater, the accession will be that of Scotland to England, just as formerly happened to Normandy, which devolved on our ancestors in the same manner and was happily added to our kingdom by hereditary right, as a rivulet to a fountain".

His words contained more than a grain of truth.

INDEX

Scotia Regnum drawn by Willem and Johan Blacu in
1635 is reproduced by kind permission of John
Bartholomew & Son Ltd., Edinburgh.